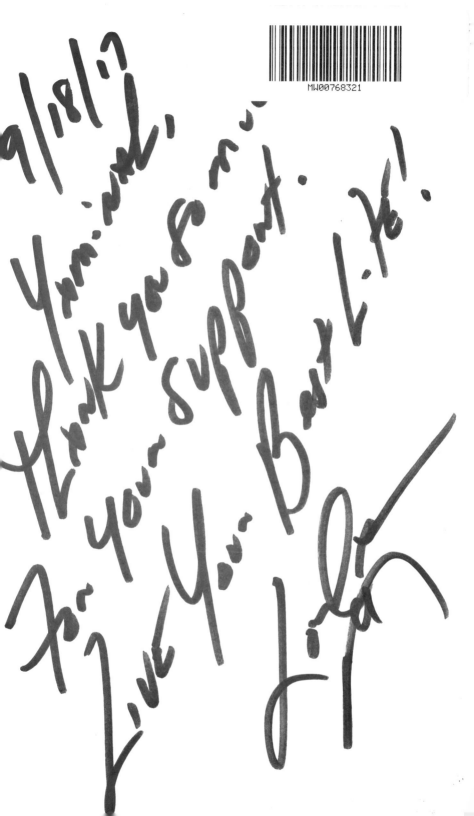

9/18/17

You...me,
thank you so much
your support.

For
Live Your Best Life!

"The two most important days of your life are the day you were born and the day you find out why." – Mark Twain

Peeling Back the Layers of Your Life

A Pathway Revealing
365 Hidden Treasures

Loronda C. Giddens

Printed in the United States of America

Published by Loronda C. Giddens

Book cover design by Loronda C. Giddens

Copyright © 2016 Loronda C. Giddens

ISBN-13: 978-0692752135

ISBN-10: 0692752137

Library of Congress Control Number: 2016915389

Inspired by

2015 GED Graduates from

The Center for Family Resources

CobbWorks Literacy Council

Paxen Learning Corporation

Youth ASSETS

Prologue

May 14, 2013 was just an ordinary work day, or so I thought. I spent the majority of the time doing my normal routine of visiting youthful offenders on my caseload. I was a juvenile probation/parole specialist who went to schools, worksites, and homes to meet with young people to ensure they were being compliant with their court orders. On this particular day, I conducted a school visit with a young man who had been kicked out of his primary high school due to frequent infractions. It was a serious situation for him because he was only two months away from graduating. I encouraged him not to give up and to enroll in a program where he can complete his coursework and walk across the stage with his peers at graduation. He knew he had to work twice as hard to accomplish his goal. I knew he could do it because he was smart like many of the young people I encountered. Most adults would have written him off because he had such a long history of criminal charges and gang involvement.

It was during another visit that he informed me he completed the required assignments, passed his final exams, and would be graduating at the end of the month. He thanked me for encouraging him and sometimes pushing him to work harder.

I was excited to hear the good news because I knew the personal struggles he had overcome. Many of the young people on my caseload have dealt with challenges you can't even begin to imagine. Yet, they still strive to have a better life despite their circumstances. This young man graduating was a big deal because rarely did I see my kids graduate. In a 15 year span, maybe ten of them reached the point of graduation. It made me feel good knowing I had made an imprint on his life. But what he probably didn't know was that he made an imprint on my life too.

After visiting with him, I went to lunch at one of my favorite places in the city. I began to think how great it would be to have a job where my primary task would involve sprinkling fairy dust and giving away gold nuggets. For me, fairy dust represents inspiration and a gold nugget represents wisdom. By all accounts I had already been doing this for years. But once I became consciously aware of what I was doing, I wanted to do it in a more intentional way. So that's what I decided I wanted to do for the rest of my life. I hope you enjoy the fairy dust and gold nuggets you receive from reading this book.

MASTER HOW YOU MOVE MOUNTAINS

You can't move a mountain if you have no vision of what's on the other side. What is the motivation to move the mountain if you don't know why you want to move it? Whenever adversity shows up on your path, and it will; you have a certain something that rises up within you that gives you the strength to move that mountain. Whenever adversity comes on my path, I automatically start to push until I get to the other side. When I was diagnosed with breast cancer in 2012 during the final year of my Master's program, I immediately started pushing because all I could see was graduation on the other side. There was no way I was going to allow anything to stop me from walking across the stage to receive my degree. From the moment I heard the words breast cancer, something activated on the inside and I instinctively knew I needed to push. I was diagnosed at Stage 0 which meant I had a couple of different routes I could choose for treatment. I knew falling apart and feeling sorry for myself wasn't an option. I knew on the other side there was a life stronger than what breast cancer tried to take. I built muscles to move mountains so when adversity comes on my path I now have the strength to push. I lived so I could share my story.

COMMIT YOURSELF TO EXCELLENCE

I learned at a very early age what it meant to be excellent. Growing up an only child, I just thought my mother was being over protective, controlling, and overbearing. But what I didn't know is that she was grooming me for excellence. I left my parent's home at 19 years old to join the United States Army where they further groomed me for excellence. When you commit yourself to excellence, you build a reputation of excellence. Underneath every fulfilled dream is the foundation of excellence.

BUILD ON YOUR SUCCESSES

Right now where you stand, you are a success. You may not believe it because by traditional standards you aren't surrounded by the **things** society deems as successful. Don't allow others to define what makes you successful. My definition of success is being the best me I can be. Being the highest expression of my potential is how I define success for myself. If you received a gold star in kindergarten and ran home to show it to your parents, you are a success. If you have triumphed in the midst of tragedies, you are a success. If you are a parent raising a child, you are a success. Don't minimize your achievements because they mean something. You already have a proven track record for success so why not continue to build on its foundation. Use your energy to continue making success happen.

WRITE A NEW CHAPTER

I spoke on the subject of teen dating violence and sex trafficking to a group of young men who were incarcerated. I'm always enlightened by something young people say. Whenever I speak, regardless of the audience I always like to know what they are thinking and feeling. The immediate feedback is good because it keeps the audience engaged and makes it interesting for everyone involved.

On this particular day it was most important because these young men were preparing to transition back into the community, re-emerging as law abiding citizens. I gave them 3 gold nuggets to focus on as they worked on their transition plan. I encouraged them to close the chapter on incarceration and write a new chapter of what they want to see for their lives. I told them they have the power within to create the life they wanted. Many of you are in the final pages of your current life chapter and are ready to write a new one. Like these young men, you may feel a sense of uncertainty of what the next chapter will be. You have the option of repeating the same chapter or stretching beyond your comfort zone to write an exciting new chapter for your life. What will you do?

LIFE IS AN ENDLESS ROAD TRIP

Daily we are faced with detours, roadblocks, wrong turns, delays, and setbacks. It surprises me sometimes how we even have a clue where we're going. Before I moved to Atlanta in '98, I studied a map just to get a clear picture of what I was about to embark upon. I had heard horror stories about the traffic and wanted to be sure about the make-up of the city. I noticed a never ending highway loop encircling Atlanta called I-285. You can easily find yourself driving on I-285 in a continuous circle if you have no idea where you are going. You can drive 285 North, 285 South, 285 East and 285 West, all on the same highway. My uncle drove around for 2 hours because he had no idea it was just a big circle. Surely there were signs along the way telling him where to go but maybe he just missed it. As an 18 year resident of the city, I still get lost from time to time but I look for the signs to guide me back to the right place. Life is no different. We have to look for the signs to guide us along our life journey. Some people will go around and around and never get off the exit to explore what's outside of their circle. Their circle represents a steady ride of comfort and predictability. But what happens when you hit a bump in the road? How do you learn to navigate through the obstacles of life if you never take a chance to explore, make mistakes, and then make corrections?

When you go on a road trip don't you pack everything you think you will need? You gas up the car, get a few of your favorite snacks and make sure the musical playlist is all set before you roll out of the driveway? I certainly do. I hop in the driver's seat of my fast car, say a prayer and I'm ready to go. On my life journey I do the same thing with one exception, God is in the driver's seat and I am the passenger. Some people put God in the passenger seat and others put God in the back seat. Then there are those who don't put God in the car at all. But one thing you will find out is that God is your life long road companion. He will be there when your finances need a complete overhaul. He will be there when you have a break down and need a mental tune up. God will go before you to change circumstances on your path and post signs leading you where to go.

NURTURE YOUR INNER SELF

There are moments in your life when you feel vibrant and everything is moving right along with ease. Then there are moments when things don't quite feel as they should. In those moments I go within to figure out how to navigate through my current state. I always lean towards something inspiring to uplift my spirits. I usually tune in to Oprah Winfrey's OWN Network, to catch an episode of Super Soul Sunday, Master Class or Lifeclass. I have endless episodes stored up on DVR so I can tap into them when I need a lift or to feel inspired. The shows are filled with people telling their life stories of how they navigate through challenging times.

Even when you aren't going through challenging times, it's nice to be able to tune into something where you feel inspired. It's nice to hear people speaking my language by echoing the things that I think. It's affirming and it makes me feel good, and feeling good is always the goal. Nurture your inner self with positive words, thoughts, and images. I tend to feel more alive when my attitude is positive regardless of what's going on in my life. Even when I was dealing with breast cancer I kept it positive because I knew it was essential for my healing. Being positive has become a way of life and it's who I have become. I wasn't always this way; I had to work hard to become the woman I am today.

MIDLIFE STAGNATION IS A REAL THING

I was speaking to a colleague who mentioned he has several friends who are currently experiencing midlife stagnation. People are reaching a point where they are questioning if this is all there is to life. Obviously there is something more to life, but how do you go about finding it? I believe in order to find out the something more, you have to take a look at yourself and decide what you are willing to do differently to make room for it.

DEVELOP DAILY RITUALS

The first thing I do when I get home from work is take a shower. I particularly enjoy a candle lit shower because it sets the tone for a relaxing evening. I'm mindful for the first few minutes of the shower to think about anything I want to get rid of that happened during my day. I visualize it being washed down the drain so I don't waste my night thinking about it. I then spend the final moments luxuriating and focusing on how the shower makes me feel. I have a wonderful oatmeal scrub which helps me to maintain my youthful glow. Prayer and meditation is also a part of my daily rituals. I often hear people say, "I can't sit still long enough to meditate" or "I get too distracted by my thoughts to meditate." I have been doing it for years and the more you do it the better at it you become, but you have to practice. You have to find moments in your day to feed your soul.

ASK YOURSELF A QUESTION:

WHAT DOES MY BEST LOOK LIKE?

Since coming up with the idea for this book, I have asked people what does your best look like. Inevitably, I get the deer in the head lights look. Then the follow up response is either, "I don't know", or "That's an interesting question" or I get no response at all. Some people will say, "I have to think about it." The whole point of me asking the question is for you to think about it. Think about your life in a way you never have before. Imagine if you were operating at the highest potential of your being, what would it look like?

USE YOUR LIFE EXPERIENCES AS

A LESSON PLAN TO TRANSFORM

Transforming your life doesn't happen on its own. Each one of you has a book's worth of life lessons you have learned. So much so, you could teach a college course all about your life. You have been given tools in the form of life experiences to assist you in the process. Apply these life experiences and transform your life. People often ask the question, "What does it mean to transform your life?" It depends on your perception of how you currently view your life. Do you feel like you need to make some changes? Do you want to pursue your life-long dream of being a business owner? Do you want to have better relationships with the people around you? The bigger question is, "What do you want and what do you need to do to get there?" If you could do it in your current state of being then you would already have what you want and be where you want to be. Since you're not quite there, then it may require a few changes here and there to get you across the finish line. But you must first have a clear vision of where you're headed.

My intention is to use my life lessons to assist others with transforming their lives. Once you are aware of the many life lessons you have learned, you can begin to put them together to make sense of your life. Once you can make sense of your life, you can begin the transformation process. Everything that's happened in my life now makes sense to me. At the time it was happening it didn't make sense. I can go back over my life and see how everything is intricately connected, nothing happened in isolation. Let's be clear, I don't want you to think you can read this book, hear me speak at conference or attend one of my workshops and think suddenly your life is transformed. It doesn't work that way. I can't transform your life for you, only you have the power to transform. I can facilitate, inspire, and empower, but only you can transform your own life. Transformation is not a quick and easy process but it is possible because people do it every day. **SPOILER ALERT:** The key to transforming your life is changing the way you think.

YOU'RE LIVING, SO LIVE

You can have more peace, more joy, and more happiness just by simply making a decision that's what you want to do. Our life is designed for us to live it in a fulfilling way. Life circumstances happen to show us we are capable of living through anything. These things aren't happening by chance. Everything in the Universe is carefully orchestrated, even the bad things. I believe some bad things happen to call us to action. If nothing happens then nothing happens. It's not until we see some atrocity on the news or hear about something terrible that we spring into action. Even in our own lives, we just go along to get along. It sometimes takes something outside of us to spark a fire within for us to move. Life is filled with wonderment but I didn't always believe it. Now I am aware and can see it for myself. I will never waste another moment of my life focusing on the negative.

MAKE AN EFFORT

What happened to the days of good customer service? I came from a corporate background where as a Customer Service Manager we would give associates awards for exemplary customer service. My mother was in the banking industry for several decades and I can remember her winning an award for the great service she provided to her clients. The award came in a classic blue box from Tiffany and it was an engraved glass star. I think subconsciously that's where my love of Tiffany began. Back then organizations took good customer service seriously but not so much anymore. Are you making an effort? Are you showing up for yourself by providing good service to yourself? Good service in the form of being the best version of yourself that you can be. It takes great effort to be your best self. Make an effort, you're worth it.

#13

LEARN HOW TO FILL YOUR OWN VOIDS

Working with young people can be
extremely rewarding and extremely disappointing
all at the same time. It's disappointing when I see
young people trying to fill the voids left behind by
an absentee father or a neglectful mother. Young
people don't know how to process the gaping
wounds of dysfunctional families, so they seek out
things to make them feel good. For a young girl it
may be an older boy who says and does nice things
for her. She is drawn to him because she doesn't
have anyone to tell her she's smart and pretty. For a
young boy, it may be joining a gang to feel a sense
of belonging. We all want to feel like we belong.
We all need to be validated. The voids we
experience as children don't go away as easily as
we may think. The voids don't go anywhere but
deeper within us so prying eyes won't see. As an
adult, we may fill the voids with one too many
glasses of wine every day when we come from
work. We may try to shop away the pain caused by
the voids. Or maybe we hang out playing slot
machines in a smoky back room of a local
convenience store. We all have ways in which we
fill the voids, bc it negative or positive we find a
way to fill the voids. I filled the void of not feeling
like I belonged by eating. Food was the only thing I

felt wouldn't reject me. I later learned how to heal the voids and no longer use food as a crutch.

LOOK AT NATURE

I have a special red cardinal who chirps outside my window and his name is Dale. I felt compelled to give him a name because he kept showing up every morning before I went to work. Sometimes I would lounge in bed and just listen, but then he started chirping so loud I had to look out of the window to see what was going on. He usually hops around on the roof, eats a few bugs then flies away after he has my full attention. I don't have any pets but Dale is like a pet I don't have to take care of. I had a bird as a child but he committed suicide by breaking his neck on the cage door. He was an unusually smart bird, he would open his bird cage and fly around the house while my parents were at work and I was at day care. The funny thing about him was he would fly back into his cage and close the door before we came home. Not sure how he did it but it was his daily ritual, his name was Starky. I love birds, rainbows, and waterfalls. If you live in Georgia or plan to visit, you may want to check out some of my favorite waterfalls; Amicalola, Duke Creek, and Anna Ruby falls.

WHEN YOU'RE READY THE

TEACHER WILL APPEAR

Before any change can take place for you to have a better life, you must first be ready for it to happen. People will say they are ready but when faced with the challenge of doing so, they get scared and go back to doing what they always do. They do so because it's comfortable and it requires little to no effort. You have to be willing to do something different. A friend of a young man I mentor asked me to help him change his life. He talked about wanting to step out of his current job as a bartender to becoming a model. He had the all of the classic features and beauty of a model but lacked confidence in his abilities. I agreed to help him by using a 90 day boot camp I designed as a result of our conversation. I gave him an idea of how the boot camp would work and he seemed excited to get started. I told him each morning he would receive an inspirational message from me to get his day started as well as a small assignment. The assignment was given as a means for him to get to know himself on a deeper level. The first day went well but the second day, not so much. He sent me a text message saying he can't do it and that I was scaring him. I thought to myself, "Why would a person be afraid of getting to know themselves?" A few months later I was sitting in a courtyard having breakfast, and a woman I met previously from a training class asked if I would be her mentor. She talked about how she wanted to lose weight and how she purposely bought a new dress several sizes smaller than her current weight to use for motivation. She mentioned aspirations of wanting to a certified trainer and other career goals. I thought I could be a source of inspiration for her, so I agreed. I told her she would have to work hard in order to achieve her goals. We exchanged contact information and I never her from her again. I do understand we all do things in our own timeframe and when you are truly ready to transform your life the teacher will appear.

BE YOURSELF

Regardless of what anyone thinks, be yourself. Whatever it looks like, be yourself. I grew up a little black girl in the suburbs listening to classic 70s and 80s rock. To this day, I still love listening to Steely Dan, Journey, REO Speedwagon, Jethro Tull, and Van Halen. I didn't care if people thought I should speak a certain way and were surprised when I didn't. I don't fit into anyone's stereotype of what they think I should be.

WHAT YOU PUT OUT YOU GET BACK

We have all heard the phrase "you reap what you sow." Think about this for a moment, what would you do if your server forgot to add something to your bill? What would you do if a cashier gave you too much money back? Do you see it as getting a gift from the Universe or as a test to do the right thing? I look at it as doing the right thing. If it doesn't belong to me then I don't want it. There have been times when a server has left off a drink from my bill and I remind them of the error. Usually they will say it's ok because it was their fault for not adding it, but I let them make the decision and not just assume its ok. I remember going to a convenience store to grab something quick and got home and realized the clerk gave me too much change back. I hopped in the car and went to the store to return the money. Most people would say what's the harm in keeping the money? I say create good karma and good karma will return to you. I live by doing the right thing, even when no one is watching. Even when you think no one is watching, someone is watching.

A GOOD MENTAL WORK

OUT IS NECESSARY

I have learned how to train my mind like an athlete trains their body. Someone once told me my mind is like a machine. I think it's important to take time out to give yourself a mental tune up whenever needed. Yoga and meditation are essential in maintaining my mental clarity and sharpness. Visualization is another form of getting a good mental work out. You have to feed your mind with what you want to see manifest in your life. What you place your attention on will multiple. Flooding your mind with positive thoughts and images increases your positive mental energy. Flooding washes away patterns of negative thinking and self-sabotaging behaviors.

SET BOUNDARIES

If you have poor boundaries then people will do what you allow. You can't get mad at them because you failed to draw the line. I found myself in patterns with people going far beyond the boundaries which I intended. But how do people know your boundaries if you don't effectively communicate them. Sometimes we feel guilty about being the perceived bad guy if we set boundaries. I'm here to tell you it's ok to set boundaries, even with family members.

TELL THE TRUTH

Lies are hard to remember but the truth will be the same 20 years from now.

DO YOUR SELF-WORK

People always ask what is self-work and where do you begin? The first thing I say is to get still and quiet your life. Remove all the distractions that keep you from spending time alone. Then start asking yourself questions that will provoke thoughts about yourself. Self-work is about getting to know yourself, not the surface you but the you that is kept hidden from the world. It can be a bit scary because you see things in yourself you don't particularly like. Once you take the first step of really understanding who you are and why you do the things you do, it will open up a whole new world. Self-work is necessary because it allows you to go back and heal old wounds, and healing old wounds is essential for real life transformation. Self-work gives you a deeper knowledge of self. I'm not saying self-work is going to be an easy process because it's not. It is a constant work that does get easier over time. Doing self-work is a new habit to be incorporated into your life. As you evolve and change, your self-work continues.

TAKE OFF THE MASK

We live in a very two-faced society. There is the
face we want the world to see and then there's the
one we keep hidden behind a mask. We all have
masks we wear for one reason or another. We wear
them because we don't people to see who we really
are, and sometimes don't want to see ourselves.
Masks show up in a variety of ways. Here are a few
of the different expressions of masks I have
encountered. **The Designer** you is the one who
always looks polished from head to toe and the only
thing you want people to see is what's on the
outside. **The Deceptive** you is the one who goes
around deceiving people on purpose just to make
yourself feel better about how empty you are inside.
The Chameleon you is the one who will be
whatever someone wants you to be in any given
situation. **The Nurturing** you is the one people
take advantage of because you have a relentless
desire for their approval. You feed on being needed
but secretly resent it when you feel like you're
being taken advantage of. **The Numb** you is the
one who has been hurt so many times in a
relationship that you no longer allow yourself to
feel because it's too painful. The danger of this is

you're so busy numbing yourself from pain, you rob yourself of feeling any pleasure and when you do feel pleasure it's only for the moment. When the moment is over you're right back to being numb again. The pretty side of ugliness is what we want the world to see. But if we have the courage to take off the mask we may discover something wonderful, the true you. **The True** you is the one who is self-aware, confident, and fearless. The mask I use to wear is hidden among these, what about you? The caveat to wearing a mask is you may not want to take it off. You become so immersed in living behind the mask that you lose sight of who you really are.

MAKE A GOOD FIRST IMPRESSION

You don't get a second chance to make a good first impression. People will remember you to the end of days if you make a good impression. They will especially remember if you make a bad impression. I would rather be known for making a good impression. It's been interesting since becoming a certified instructor and seeing former students who attended one of my training classes. Most will tell me something they remembered from the class. I like to leave them with gold nuggets in addition to the instructional material. One guy walked up and said, "I remember you, you are a great motivator." It makes me feel good to know something I said made an impression, more importantly a good impression.

YOUR DREAMS ARE REAL

Your dreams have a direct connection to your purpose. No matter what was going on in my life, my dream was still inside of me alive and kicking. No breast cancer diagnosis, no depression, no midlife stagnation, no financial concerns could stop me from believing in my dreams. It's not always easy to believe in your dreams, especially when the people around you don't believe in your dreams. I started to wonder if it was important for anyone outside of me to believe in my dreams. The answer for me was no because they are my dreams and not anyone else's. All too often when you tell people your dreams, they will either try to talk you out of it or give you so much negative feedback that you abandon your dreams. Be careful who you share your dreams with because there are dream slayers out there just waiting to kill your dreams.

NO MORE NEW YEAR'S RESOLUTIONS

Have you noticed every January you start to see commercials for gym memberships and different weight loss programs to encourage people to keep their new year's resolutions? I drove past a gym near my house and it appeared every parking spot was filled. A few months later people fell off and the parking lot wasn't as full. People forgot about their resolutions and went back to their old ways. Every day you wake up you have a new opportunity to do something different. You can simply press the reset button and start over. You don't have to wait until a certain time of year. Set the intention of what you want to do and do it.

READ MORE

In my early twenties my best friend Jennifer introduced to a book called the *"The Celestine Prophecy"* by author James Redfield. I believe this book played an integral role in my spiritual awakening. Years later, I had an opportunity to meet Mr. Redfield at my church and told him what an imprint his book made on my life. It opened something inside of me I didn't know existed. He gave me a signed copy of his book to which I gave to a young man who was going to prison. I told him not to give up hope and to read the book because it may change his life.

PLAY AND HAVE FUN

Do some things you used to enjoy when you were kids. One of my fondest childhood memories was flying kites with my dad for hours. I enjoy it so much that I still do it whenever the mood hits. I was in Puerto Rico a few years ago and came across a big open field, near the Castillo de San Cristobal Fort in San Juan. People were flying kites and little children were running around having fun. A local vendor was selling kites nearby and I couldn't resist the urge to buy my own to fly. I will always cherish the memory of my dad and me flying kites together.

MAKE SOMEONE'S DAY

I was at home recovering from a bad cold, the flu, or allergies. I didn't know what it was but I felt awful. The only thing I wanted to do was watch something mindless on television when my phone rang. I answered, and on the other end of the phone was a sweet little voice singing my favorite song. It was my Director's son, Cole Justice singing Ed Sheeran's *"Thinking Out Loud."* Neither Cole nor his mother knew how much it made my day. A few months earlier, I had the pleasure of meeting this handsome 6 year old. He has the most soulful brown eyes I have ever seen. When I met him I asked for a hug, and he gladly obliged. I said, "I 'm going to take you home with me." He looked up at his mom as if to say, is it ok? I then said, "I have a pool and you can come over to go swimming." He replied, "I don't know how to swim." I said, "It was ok I will teach you." He leaned over and put his little head on my shoulder and my heart melted.

#29

SHOW YOUR PERSONALITY

I can't recall the day when I knew I was funny. I've always known myself to be quick witted, having a fast response whenever needed. Being funny I guess has been a natural progression to really show itself in a big way. Someone told me once they like being around me because I am funny and silly. It was sort of surprising coming from this person because they never show any emotion. You can't tell if they are enjoying themselves or not, so how would I know I'm being funny and silly. I'm just being me. Others have told me I'm funny and will pretty much say and do anything, within reason of course. I don't intentionally go around doing or saying things to hurt people. I believe in saying what I feel. If you don't want the truth then I may not be the girl you ask. I had a co-worker tell me that she has to channel her inner Loronda when faced with something difficult. She calls me fearless. I told her, "Channel your inner you because you are fearless too."

#30

SHOW YOUR APPRECIATION

I was coming out of my favorite bagel spot one morning on my way to work and noticed an older gentleman making his way in as I was walking out. He walked with a cane, as he slowly approached the entryway of the building. I patiently stood by with a smile as I held the door open, waiting for him to walk through. He thanked me for holding door and said, "I appreciate your smile." I said, "Thank you and have a nice day." If someone does something nice for you, show them your appreciation.

#31

ACCEPT HELP

It was challenging for me to accept help after I was diagnosed with breast cancer. I was so accustomed to doing everything myself. One thing I do know is you can't do everything. You need people to help you to get things done. My mother always taught me to be independent but there are limits to what you can and can't do by yourself.

BE FLEXIBLE

Being flexible wasn't as easy for me as it appeared to be. I grew up in a very structured environment where everything had to be a certain way. Then I joined the military which only further enhanced my inflexibility. I always admired people who seemingly flew by the seat of their pants to do things spontaneously. I went Jamaica in the late 90s with a written agenda in hand of everything I wanted to do. Each day was planned out weeks in advance. I had to laugh at myself when I got there because who goes on vacation with a written agenda. Isn't the whole point of being away from your workplace is to be free of agendas.

YOUR THOUGHTS ARE CONTROLLING

Every day we wake up we hit the play button on some intrusive thought from our past or our now that we can't seem to let go. It plays all day long as if it were the soundtrack of our lives. It may be thoughts like "you will never amount to anything" or "you're not pretty enough" or "you have low self-esteem" or "you're just like your dead beat father" or "I don't deserve to be happy" or "I'm worthless." These thoughts are intrusive, controlling, and debilitating but more importantly these thoughts are false. These thoughts are not a true representation of who we are, yet somehow we were taught to believe them. We all have thoughts which dishonor and devalue our worth. It's important to be aware of their existence because awareness is the first step in extinguishing these thoughts. You have the power to control your thoughts but it takes a lot of practice.

TRUST YOURSELF

We are quick to trust others more than we trust ourselves. Can you count on yourself not to let yourself down? Can you trust your thoughts and ideas? Do you value others opinions over your own? Their opinion is no more important than your own.

NEVER LET PEOPLE SEE YOU SWEAT

Since becoming a public speaker, I'm often asked if I get nervous about speaking in front of people. My usual response is no. Being in front of people and saying something to potentially change someone's life is very empowering. I advise others who are interested in public speaking never let people see you sweat. Even if you are falling apart on the inside maintain yourself on the outside.

JUST BE

I was speaking with an older lady while waiting to check out in a retail store and the cash register was starting to slow down. The cashier kept apologizing for the delay. The woman said, "That's ok baby I'm in no hurry, I will just be until it's my time." Then she turned to me and said, "I try to tell young people all the time to slow down and just be but they are always in a hurry." She went on to say, "My momma told me a long time ago not to worry about things you can't change."

#37

DON'T WORRY ABOUT

THINGS YOU CAN'T CHANGE

Growing up I would always tell my mother not to worry about things you can't change. She was a worrier, she worried about everything. She always worried that something would happen to me if she let me go somewhere out of her supervision. My mindset was if something was going to happen it would occur at any time. Life circumstances will happen regardless of how much preparation we do to avoid it. You can't change any situation by worrying.

#38

GET PASSIONATE ABOUT YOUR LIFE

Living life passionately is a choice. Living a passionate life means you are pursuing your dreams and living your purpose. I know it's easier said than done because most people are merely existing in the world. When I hear the word passion, I think of a burning desire for something. I have a burning desire to be the best me I can be. There was a time when I was passionate about dwelling in darkness. I was merely existing and not really living. I woke up one day and decided I wanted to be happy. I had been so unhappy for such a long time it just felt normal. I was willing to do the hard work to turn my life around.

#39

TRY SOMETHING NEW

What's the worst thing that could happen?
You may find out that you actually liked it or you
may not. At least you can make an informed
decision about not doing it again. I met a 16 year
old girl who said she doesn't like change and doesn't
like to try anything new. When offered a piece of
candy, she declined and asked her best friend to try
the candy on her behalf. Her best friend tried it and
told her she would like it. I began to wonder what
happened in her short life to make her so resistant to
trying something new. Then I wondered if she
would go through her entire life trusting someone
else's opinion instead of her own.

My interaction with her reminded me of a
time when I was resistant to trying anything new. I
would only eat what my mother cooked and nothing
else. If she didn't cook it, I didn't eat it. My friend
Mia from high school introduced me to Jamaican
food and the spicy flavors completely opened up my
taste buds. It was a great precursor for when I
traveled throughout Europe while in the Army. I
learned to embrace the foods of other cultures. I'm
a complete foodie who enjoys Thai, Mexican,
Cuban, Peruvian, Italian and basically anything with
an amazing flavor. I have developed a sophisticated
and discriminating palate for good food.

#40

THERE ARE NO SHORTCUTS

Whatever it is you want to achieve, understand there are no shortcuts. I watched my parents get up every day and go to work to achieve what they wanted. They never took shortcuts, they never looked for shortcuts; they just worked hard. They built a solid foundation for me to stand on which gave me the opportunity to pursue my dreams. I developed my work ethic by watching them.

#41

IF YOU WANT THINGS TO BE
DIFFERENT THEN YOU HAVE
TO DO SOMETHING DIFFERENT

After graduating with a Master of Arts in Forensic Psychology, I had the expectation that I could work anywhere I wanted. I applied to every organization with an acronym you can think of; the FBI, CIA, DHS, and so on and so on. I didn't so much as receive a rejection letter from the majority of the agencies and when I did, it read something like "your qualifications don't meet our preferred qualifications." In most cases I did meet the preferred qualifications or I wouldn't have wasted time completing a mountain of paperwork to do the application. After about six months I decided to stop sending out resumes to anyone who was hiring. I thought about it for a moment and it became obvious I should be doing something different. I didn't know what the something different would be, but I became still so it would become obvious to me how the something different would manifest in my life.

About three months later, I received an email from a colleague who was looking for presenters to speak to a group of GED students during their professional development week. I was accustomed to speaking in front of young people in a group setting but nothing in such a formal way. I can recall sitting in my office and saying to myself after reading the email, "Loronda, you have to do something different if you want something different." I called my colleague to get further details and agreed to be one of the presenters. I prepared for my talk by doing a presentation on goal setting. It was a great experience because I felt like the young people were engaged, which is sometimes a difficult thing to achieve. They came up afterwards to ask questions and give me a hug to thank me for the presentation. A few days later, I knew this was the something different I was supposed to be doing. Receiving the email from my colleague, Granville Freeman changed the trajectory of where I thought I wanted to go to where I was meant to be.

#42

DON'T LET SOMEONE

BORROW YOUR FAVORITE THING

When I was a kid, I loved riding my bike from sun up to sun down in the summertime. Dirt bikes were real popular with the kids in my neighborhood, and I had my eye on a new girl version of a really cool dirt bike. It was a pink Huffy Sweet Thunder 2. My parents surprised me with a shiny new one on Christmas morning. A few days after riding my new bike around and showing it off to everyone, a kid I knew asked if he could take it for spin. I agreed but told him to just ride it to the corner and back. Little did I know he had plans to take my bike for a real spin. He rode to the corner, passed the corner and kept going. He didn't come back for hours. I was so upset. I was I thinking didn't want my parents to know I let someone ride my bike. He eventually showed up and left the bike in my front yard. Let it be a lesson to you; don't let someone borrow your favorite thing.

I CAN DO MORE BUT I CHOSE TO DO LESS

Throughout my life I have had moments when I decided to be nothing more than average. It was safe, it was comfortable and I didn't have to put forth much effort. I was living on a low frequency. A series of inspiration hit and I decided there was nothing good about being average. I went from being a C student in high school to graduating Magna Cum Laude at the university. I turned up the volume on my life and started living on a higher frequency.

BE KIND TO YOURSELF

We have a tendency of treating others better than we treat ourselves. If you're doing this please stop. No one deserves to be treated better than you treat yourself. It's not selfish to treat yourself well. Take yourself out on dates if you don't have anyone to go out with. There's nothing wrong with walking into a restaurant and proudly asking for a table for one, I do it all the time. I just so happen to be one of those people who enjoys their own company. Send yourself some flowers or my personal favorite, buy yourself some Tiffany jewelry. On Valentine's Day instead of dreading it, send yourself a nice card in the mail and get together with some of your other single friends and celebrate.

#45

SET YOUR SOUNDTRACK FOR THE DAY

I wake up singing a different song every day, and throughout the day I listen to music because it makes me feel good. I usually listen to something from the 80s or 90s, a time when artist sang songs with meaning. On my way in to work I listen to old school hip hop and in the evening is talk radio or jazz to wind down from the day. I grew up with music as I'm sure many of you did. Waking up early on a Saturday morning to clean the house; listening to favorites like Earth, Wind and Fire, The O'Jays, and The Commodores. I loved music so much that I would stay up all night listening to the radio. I called the radio station to request my favorite song and talk to the deejay. It didn't matter if I had school the next day or not. It was one of my favorite things to do until my aunt told my mom she heard me talking on the radio in the middle of the night. My favorite pastime came to a screeching halt. Music was the one thing to soothe my aching soul and got me through my childhood.

While writing this book I had a soundtrack which is odd because normally I like it quiet when I'm writing. I listened to Loose Ends who I consider to be one of the greatest R&B groups to come out of the United Kingdom. I wish the original group would get back together to make new

music and go on tour. Wishful thinking, but at least
they left behind a catalog of great music.

BELIEVE YOUR LIFE CAN BE MAGICAL

The miracle of child birth is nothing more than magical. We can recapture the magic just by the way we perceive our lives. I haven't always been as positive, optimistic, or even excited about seeing a new day. The moments I have experienced over the last few years have been nothing short of magical. When you believe, the treasures of your life are no longer hidden. The revealed treasures will guide you along your life path to your highest good and greatest joy. You will suddenly start to see your dreams come true. The key to unlocking the door to your dreams is within your reach. Grab the key, unlock the door and boldly walk in to receive your treasures.

GIVE UP YOUR 5 YEAR PLAN

I made a 5 year plan over ten years ago and nothing on the 5 year plan came to fruition in that time frame. The only two items listed on the plan I can recall is to get my master's degree and to get a certification in massage therapy. I'm not saying to abandon your dreams but what I am saying is your dreams don't have an expiration date on them. Look at your dreams to see how they are tied to your purpose. Not everything on your 5 year plan is tied to your purpose. A certification in massage therapy had absolutely nothing to do with my purpose. I'm glad I didn't waste the time or money pursuing it. Pace yourself because your dreams don't happen when you think they should. We get so caught up in meeting certain goals by a certain time that we miss the journey of getting there.

#48

SHARE YOUR STORY

I'm not telling you what I think; I'm telling you what I know. I have lived each and every one of these 365 lessons. Everyone has their own lessons to learn at their own pace. My intention is for people to benefit from what I've learned. We can help each other to have a more meaningful existence when we share our stories. There is power in telling your story, power for you because you make a difference in someone's life, and power for someone else because they are inspired to do something different. I was talking to a young lady who was incarcerated on a pretty serious offense. I encouraged her to share her story with her peers when she is released, with the hope it would encourage them not to travel down the same road of incarceration. Despite her circumstances, she is hopeful, she writes amazing poetry, she is intelligent, she seeks motivation and she aspires to be an inspirational speaker. She wants her voice to be heard. What are you doing with your story? Are you ashamed of your story and hiding it from the world or are you using it to inspire others. I don't know about you but I'm using my story to inspire others.

BE TRANSPARENT

A woman came up to me after a speaking engagement and said you were so transparent. It was as if she were surprised I would be that way. Honestly at this stage in my life I don't know any other way to be but myself. What you see is what you get. But don't be confused about what you think you see. I may appear one way but the layers do run deep. You have to get to know me to understand the depth of the layers. It's not that complicated. At least I don't think so. I'm a sweet introvert who enjoys quiet times alone more than large noisy group settings. But I absolutely feed off the energy of the crowd when I'm doing speaking engagements. I prefer one on one meaningful conversations over random small talk. I'm not easily impressed but can get excited about the smallest of things. Just because I'm an introvert, don't mistake me for being shy because I'm not. Sometimes we dismiss people because they are too complicated but you may be missing out on someone who may be worth your time.

HELP EACH OTHER TO FUFILL DREAMS

If there is something you can do to help someone fulfill their dreams then do it. All too often I hear people say they want to help you get to the next level but when you call on them they fail to respond. I understand people say things in the moment and it sounds good in that moment. I see it occurring a lot when people are networking. Most times it's all talk and no action. I feel like if you're not genuinely interested in helping a person then you shouldn't make an offer if you don't really mean it. I attended a conference about a year ago and was talking to the keynote speaker afterwards to express my interest in public speaking. He said he was looking to put together a team of speakers who would go around the world spreading hope. I thought what a great idea because that's exactly what I want to do. I told him I would love to hear more and would be interested in joining the team. He requested for me to send him an email with my contact information and he would get back to me to discuss the new venture. Needless to say, I never heard anything from him. I don't listen to what people say I look at what they actually do. Actions speak louder than words.

#51

MAKE A DIFFERENCE

If you can do something to make a difference in the world then do it. If you can do something to make a difference in someone's life then do it. Each and every one of us has a purpose which is connected to the greater good of humanity.

#52

ALLOW YOURSELF TO FEEL

All too often we go through life not feeling anything. Some people check out in the feeling department and never check back in.   There is always a risk of getting hurt but if you never feel you will never feel. Don't allow past experiences to take away your ability to feel. For some it's painful to feel and it was for me too. Now it's a good feeling to feel. I want to feel every aspect of life regardless of the risk of being hurt. I don't feel alive unless I am feeling something. Anytime I do a speaking engagement, it is always my intention for the audience to feel something. The energy I feel in return from them is indescribable. We laugh, we cry, we feel.

#53

KNOW WHAT MAKES YOU HAPPY

     I find it interesting how easily we are able to define what we don't want and have so much trouble defining what we do want. You know when you are unhappy but can't quite put your finger on what makes you happy. Is it that we just don't think about it or is it not important. People say they want to be happy but they don't know where to start. The first thing you do is give some serious thought about what will make you happy. The next step is deciding what you are willing to do to get to your happy place. Being happy is a decision and it requires you to do something. Sometimes you may know what it takes to make you happy but don't have the willingness to see it through. Happiness is a state of mind regardless of the outer appearance of your life. I refuse to spend another second of my life being unhappy. Been there, done that, and purchased the unhappy t-shirt.

MAKE POWER MOVES

This was my mantra for 2014 and boy did I make some power moves. I saw these words on the front cover of Oprah's magazine so I clipped it out and placed it on my vision board. Something about those words took a hold of me and didn't let go. By the way, I'm still making power moves.

#55

BE YOUR BEST YOU

When you are being the best you that you can be, you will attract what you want. I worked hard to get my advance degrees not only as a means to move forward in my career but as a means of validation. Not validation for anyone else but for myself. It made me feel good to work towards something no one can ever take away from me. It adds value to my self-worth, my self-esteem, and my self-confidence which helps me to be the best me I can be. Society tells us that acquiring material possessions is the definition of success. I believe being my best self is a success.

#56

RECOGNIZE LIFE CYCLES

If we don't learn the life lessons as they
show up on our path, we are doomed to repeat them
over and over again. Have you ever been in a
relationship with someone and it didn't work out?
We all have experienced this at least once or twice
or maybe even ten times. You meet the next person
but you have the same experience with them as you
did the last person. And the same thing keeps
happening. At some point you may want to stop
and look at the situation and ask yourself some
questions. You meet different people but keeping
having the same experiences. It could be a life
cycle of having dysfunctional relationships. You
didn't recognize the life cycle because by all
accounts what you knew about relationships was
good. You didn't recognize the life cycle of
dysfunction so it kept repeating itself. You
probably told your friends you keep meeting the
same person but with a different face. Maybe there
was a lesson to learn with the first person you met.
You didn't learn the lesson so it repeated itself. I
feel like people come into your life for certain
reasons. Sometimes there is a lesson for you to
learn or maybe the lesson is for the other person.
But the common denominator in all of your
relationships is you.

LOOK UP AND LOOK AROUND

Every morning on my way to work I usually take the same route. I see the same billboards but never really paying too much attention to them. One day as I sipped on my favorite cup of coffee I noticed one billboard in particular. It was as if it jumped out in front of my car because I had been ignoring it for so long. It was an advertisement for a local hospital. A nurse was at the bed side of her patient, and above her head were the words "we are life changers." Something about those words resonated and I began to think about the work I do with young people. I smiled to myself and said, "You are a life changer." A few months went by and the sign changed, it was the same hospital advertisement but this time the words read, "We are healers." I smiled to myself once again as I thought about my young people. I witnessed breakthroughs as we spent countless hours talking about their lives. I began the journey of healing the teenage girl in me as a result of my interaction with them. Each of us has the ability to heal others and change lives. When trying to figure out what your purpose is in life, look up and look around for the answer. It's literally right in front of you.

KNOW WHO ARE YOU

WITHOUT THE THINGS

When you are living your purpose all things will be added to you, but if those things should happen to go away you will still have your purpose. Are you defined by what you have or are you defined by the type of person you are? When Hurricane Katrina hit New Orleans in 2005, it changed my whole outlook on how I saw material things. People were standing on the rooftops of their homes screaming to be rescued. For many, having someone come to their rescue was the most important thing. Devastation rolled through the city and people were stripped of irreplaceable family heirlooms they can never recover. Witnessing such loss and human suffering changed me, as it did many people around the nation; especially the people of New Orleans.

FIND YOUR SOURCE OF INSPIRATION

Find it and repeat it over and over because you're going to need it. Sometimes we find ourselves feeling uninspired. In those moments we have to know where to go to draw out inspiration. Inspiration doesn't operate in a vacuum, you don't just find it once and it's done. Finding your source of inspiration is ongoing. You may have multiple sources and you will use them all to keep you inspired when you need it the most. I am very aware when I'm not feeling inspired. In the past it was easy for depression to set in to render me inactive.

My sources of inspiration are prayer, mediation, music, and television programming with inspirational messages. I also tap into nature by opening my window first thing in the morning to hear the birds singing to feel inspired. We are surrounded by inspiration and all we have to do is connect to it.

In June of 2015, I realized I had lost my inspiration. I took a few days off from work just so I could focus my attention on inspiration. I meditated and prayed 3 times a day for 3 days and read the first 3 chapters of Dr. Wayne Dyer 's book, "Inspiration: Your Ultimate Calling." Dr. Dyer reminded me that inspiration comes from within, to be in spirit with God. Ever since then inspiration has been pouring out of me.

#60

GOD IS AN ARTIST

I am in awe!

Have you ever looked up at the sky on any given day? What do you see? Sometimes I see brushstrokes across the sky. Sometimes the sunrise looks like an egg sizzling sunny side up in hot a skillet across the morning sky. Other times the sunset is a calming end to a perfect day. I often find myself pulling over on the side of the road to capture a photo of the art in the sky. Most of the time I'm on my way to work or on my way home from work. I have countless images of the beautiful works designed by God. The cover for Peeling Back the Layers was taken as I was driving home from work one afternoon. I turned the corner heading towards the highway and before me was the most beautiful rainbow I had ever seen. I feel like God communicates to me through his many images in the sky. He has my full attention with His skillful artwork. He obviously knows I'm an art lover because He does paintings in the sky just for me.

BE PATIENT

It took me some time to figure out that everything doesn't happen when I want it. There were times when I wanted to hurry through certain periods in my life to get to a place I thought I wanted to be. We live in such a microwave society of having everything thing we want when we want it. We have access to whatever we want at the tip of our fingers. Swipe left or swipe right, click and point, and voila there it is. We have been conditioned to believe we don't have to wait for anything. The concept of waiting has become so foreign. It wasn't until I had no choice but to wait is when I truly understood what it meant. I was patiently waiting for God to move in my life in a major way. But what I didn't know is He was waiting patiently on me to be still long enough so He could.

#62

LISTEN FOR THE ANSWERS

The beauty of my mornings is hearing the birds serenading a new day. It's a time when I receive many of the answers to the questions I am seeking. I have learned to get still, get quiet, and listen for the answers. I may go to sleep with a question on my mind and as I awake the answer is revealed to me. I give myself time in the morning to receive a download of information. I consult with God on **EVERYTHING**. I listen not only with my ears but my entire body. I receive information from the quiet space within as well as from the noisiness of the atmosphere. You would be surprised to know how many answers to your life questions are right in front of you if only you paid attention.

AWARENESS IS THE KEY

I love quotes and post them everywhere in any office space I occupy. This has been ongoing since the late eighties when I worked in the corporate sector. Before making my transition from corporate in 2001 I received a gift. I was sitting at my desk one day and was led to draw six arrows in an ascending position on a little sticky note. I had no clue what it meant but I knew enough to keep the small piece of paper. I left it on my desk for several days and stared at it to see if anything would reveal itself, it didn't immediately. I took the paper home with the hopes something would come into my awareness. It wasn't until about several months later that I started to see the magic happening. I created the quote, "Realization is the first step to change, once you learn to embrace change you are able to move forward." I thought the quote was so good I did a copyright in 2003 with the Library of Congress just in case. I didn't know at the time what the six arrows meant but now I do and you're going to love it. This book is an example of my awareness and willingness to embrace change. The more you become aware the more you will see. Your spiritual insight will increase and you will see things you've never seen before. A secret passageway has been opened and I can see things that was already there.

#64

LAYERS COVER YOUR LIFE PURPOSE

Layers manifest itself as guilt, shame, fear, lack of confidence, procrastination, other people's expectations, self-loathing and an unwillingness to change. This isn't a comprehensive list because we are faced with different types of layers that challenge us. But it's a good start for understanding the existence of layers. Being aware they exist is a huge step in the right direction to begin peeling. We may see layers as a normal part of who we are, so the need to peel them may not be the first thing we think about doing. Let me assure you that peeling my own layers hasn't been the most comfortable thing I've ever done. It was painful because I had to take a deep look at myself and see myself for the first time in a real way. It was painful because I had to go back to the layers place of origin and work my way forward. Peeling back the layers is a lesson in awareness, healing, and transformation. You may feel you are at a crossroads and know there is more to life than what you're currently experiencing. You may be questioning what your life purpose is and what you came here to do. Start by peeling back the layers of your life because your purpose is buried underneath the layers.

WE ARE BORN INTO LAYERS

So now that we know about layers, where do they come from? Layers often exist before we even grace the planet with our presence. Think about the many secrets families hide about a child's birth. I heard a story about a guy who wondered his entire life about the man who was his father. He didn't find out until adulthood that the man living across the street most of his life was his father. Everyone in the family knew but they kept the secret from him. He often tried to fill the void of his absentee father with reckless self-sabotaging behavior. He turned out to be the exact thing in his children's life, an absentee father. His children would see him every now and then but not enough to actually say he's raising his children. The void his father created by not being there is the same void he created in his own children. The cycle just continues until someone in the cycle recognizes it as such and decides to peel the layer. A dysfunctional relationship with a parent sets the tone for every relationship going forward. Sometimes we recognize the layers but would rather keep them because they feel comfortable.

REPLACE YOUR NEGATIVE

THOUGHTS WITH POSITIVE THOUGHTS

One of the main factors in transforming your life is to be mindful of your thoughts. There was a time when most of my thoughts were negative ones. Negative thoughts makes you feel bad, at least it did for me. Negative thoughts are a breeding ground for depression. The best way to replace your negative thoughts with positive thoughts is to practice. Fake it until you make it. After a while the negative thoughts will flee because they can't stand being in a place where positivity is happening. Positive thoughts and negative thoughts have difficulty occupying the same space. Being and thinking positive will always win.

KNOW THE DIFFERENCE BETWEEN A

JOB, A CAREER, AND YOUR PURPOSE

A job is something you do, a career is something you achieve, and your purpose is who you are with every fiber of your being. Your purpose is what you came here to do. We all came here with an assignment to fulfill. Some people know from birth exactly what they are supposed to do and they go about doing it almost immediately. Others of us eventually figure it out, and then sadly there are those who never fulfill their purpose. The graveyard is filled with people who never discovered they had a purpose let alone fulfilled it. If you want to know your purpose, then ask.

#68

ASK YOURSELF A QUESTION: AM I

LIVING A DREAM OR A NIGHTMARE?

One day I asked a co-worker how she was doing and she said "I am living the dream." I thought about it for a moment because the words just resonated in my spirit. I smiled and told her I was planning to use those words whenever someone asked me how I was doing. I love the implication of the words "I am living the dream." My dream is to go around the world to use my voice to inspire others to transform the lives and live their dreams. Many people are afraid to live their dream, either because they don't think it's possible or they can't see the vision of how it can happen. You have dreams so that you can fulfill your purpose. Your dreams are just a visual image of your purpose. When you're living a nightmare of fear, anxiety, and despair, it's difficult to imagine how living a dream is possible. It takes consistent belief every single day that living your dream can be your reality.

BE IN THE MOMENT

Being in the moment is the only moment we have, yesterday is gone, and tomorrow isn't here yet.

HAVE THE COURAGE TO

LIVE WHAT YOU BELIEVE

Whatever you believe, have the courage to live it. I knew someone who believed very strongly in her relationship with God but was too afraid to allow herself to live what she believed. She would pray often, meditate regularly, and would go to church to worship most Sundays. When she wasn't at church on Sunday, she would tune in online as well as attend classes during the week. We would have great conversations about the power of God and how you can transform your life if only you would surrender and be obedient to His will. Here in lies the challenge. She completely understood what to do and how to do it but was afraid. The surrender part is the challenge because once you surrender to doing things God's way you can no longer do things the way you were doing them. You can because you have free will. But once you make the commitment you have to follow through. A young man I mentored once told me the reason he tends to get stuck is because he's afraid of disappointing God. I can usually tell when it's happening and will remind him of his greatness, and tell him how much God loves him.

ALLOW YOURSELF TO

LOVE AND BE LOVED

During the month of February, I have numerous speaking engagements with young people in recognition of Teen Dating Violence Awareness and Prevention month. We start out talking about their relationship with their peers. Then we talk about the warnings signs of dating violence and possible reasons why it happens. Towards the end of the presentation we talk about the traits of unhealthy versus healthy relationships. I usually ask them, "Who is the first person they ever loved?" Inevitably, I will hear mom, dad or both parents. Then I ask, "What happens if you have a bad relationship with the first person you ever loved? Everyone in the rooms usually says, "You will have bad relationships with others." How do you know how to love if the love you know is the result of a bad relationship with a parent? How do you allow yourself to love if you don't know what love is? People give love based on how they know to give it but may not know how they need to receive it. I was watching an episode of Super Soul Sunday and Oprah was interviewing one of my favorite spiritual teachers, Gary Zukav who is the author of *"The Seat of the Soul."* Oprah asked him what was the most difficult lesson he ever learned, he thought about it for a moment and then he said, "Love." In one of the teen dating violence talks, one of the young men described love as confusing. I told him love is confusing but it can also be rewarding if you allow yourself to love and be loved." Before you can love anyone else you must first love yourself and know how you need to be loved.

CREATE AN INTENTIONAL VISION BOARD

Facilitating vision board events has become one of my favorite things to do. College professors, non-profit organizations, elementary, and high schools have asked me to speak about vision boards and to teach others how to create their own. I enjoy teaching about vision boards because it's been phenomenal for me to see the things on my vision board manifest in my life. I usually bring my vision board with me when I speak to show people how magical it can be. The most fun I ever had was when I spoke with one hundred fifth graders at Dowell Elementary. I talked to them for about 45 minutes on the importance of setting goals then we spent another hour doing vision boards. I was amazed at how the little people sat still for almost 2 hours. We had fun high fiving each other and laughing about silly things. I invited my mentee to come along to assist and when he walked in the room the kids were so excited because they thought he was Usher. We walked around talking to the kids about their goals, dreams, and aspirations as they worked on the vision boards. One little boy's vision board was filled with soccer balls, soccer clothes, and soccer players. I asked him, "What he wanted to do when he grew up?" He said, "A soccer player because my daddy told me I can do anything I want to do if I work hard." It made me smile that this little guy knew exactly what he wanted to do without question.

For those who don't know what a vision board is or never heard of one. It's a poster, cork board, or anything you can paste things on that you want to manifest in your life. Vision boards are designed to do exactly what it implies, to have a vision or to visualize. Vision boards are an expression of your wildest dreams connecting to your purpose. It doesn't have to be only pictures. I'm a word girl so I have very few pictures on my vision board. The exciting thing about vision boards is, if you put some intention behind it during its creation; you will begin to see exactly what you want. What we place our attention on expands and it keeps expanding. It's fine to put material things on your vision board but I steer clear of them. I believe if I am living my purpose, all of the material things I want will show up.

On my vision board you will see my books as best sellers. I also have the words Amazon.com. I knew I wanted to sell through Amazon but I didn't know it would be self-published through them as well. I have a picture of myself standing at a podium in front of a huge audience handing out gold nuggets. I have a quote by Ralph Waldo Emerson that says, "Today is a new day. You shall begin it well and serenely and too high a spirit to be cumbered with your old nonsense." When I saw the quote in O magazine, I knew it had to be on my vision board. I was still dwelling in some old nonsense. I looked at the quote every single day and knew I had to do something different. Sometimes you just need something different to focus your energy on. Vision boards are real and they have energy. I had a friend who reluctantly went to a vision board party in January 2014. She put on her vision board that she wanted to have a new relationship, go to Fiji, and to eat better to aid with losing weight. In the same year she lost 20 pounds, she was engaged to be married, and went to Fiji. Even she couldn't believe how her life had been transformed. Do yourself a favor and create an intentional vision board. It's an accountability tool to keep you focused on your goals. Place it somewhere you can view it daily.

#73

IT JUST KEEPS GETTING BETTER

God has a golden light shining on my path.
It's my guide to show me where He wants me to go.
Every day it just keeps getting better and brighter.

I FEEL GOOD WHEN (fill in the blank)

I feel good when I hear birds singing at morning rise. I feel good when I hear children laughing for no reason at all. I feel good when I hear good music. I feel good when I know I have made a difference. I feel good when I can put my feet up and relax. I feel good when I meditate. I feel good when I'm riding my bike. I feel good when I had my convertible and the top was down and the wind was blowing in my face. I feel good when I wake up to see another day. I feel good when I have a fun day at work. I feel good when I make someone laugh. I feel good when sipping on well-mixed Margarita (Grand Marnier, top shelf Tequila, freshly squeezed lime juice, on the rocks with a salted rim). I feel good when sitting on the back of a catamaran watching the sun melt into the ocean. I feel good when I reminisce about the fun times I had in the Army. I feel good after taking a long hot shower. I feel good when I'm writing. When do you feel good?

#75

PEEL BACK THE LAYERS OF YOUR LIFE

World renowned artist Michelangelo said this about one of his most notable works of art, "David was always there in the marble. I just took away everything that wasn't David." Build up the courage you need to be your own Michelangelo and take away everything that isn't you. Peel back the layers of your life to reveal your masterpiece within. I stood in the Louvre Museum in Paris at the tender age of 20 years old gazing up at the statue of David. I had no idea I was embarking upon the journey of peeling back the layers of my own life.

STOP DRIVING YOUR CAR

LOOKING IN THE REARVIEW MIRROR

The past is the past and all you have is this moment. What story are you leading with that is a reflection of what you have experienced in your past. I was listening to a young woman on a talk show who was having issues with her boyfriend of 6 months. Her leading story to the host was that she was cheated on by every boyfriend in her past. She felt she had to monitor him and constantly question him so he didn't cheat on her. Newsflash, if someone is going to cheat on you they will do it regardless of how much you monitor their activities. Our past behaviors have a tendency to dictate what our present behaviors will be. It doesn't have to be that way because we do possess the power to change the narrative, if we choose. We can't go back and undo what's already been done. If you look in your rearview mirror and all you see is pain, look a little closer to see the triumph.

TAKE THE RISK

Don't allow fear to stop you from taking the risk. Take the risk to breathe instead of being suffocated by a life with no meaning.

"And the day came when the risk to remain tight in a bud was more painful than the risk it took to blossom." - Anais Nin

BE CONFIDENT

On the days you don't feel confident, wear it anyway. Put on the clothes of a confident person in the morning before you leave the house. The more you wear confidence the more you begin to feel it. I was well into my forties before I truly felt confident. I had moments of confidence here and there but it doesn't happen until you get to an age where you can fully understand and appreciate it. Confidence feels like freedom, it feels like validation, it feels like empowerment, it feels like a super hero, and it feels like you can conquer the world. I know it's a real feeling because I've never felt it before. The greatest part of all about feeling confident is no one can take it from me and I am certainly no longer giving it away.

SETBACKS ARE A SET UP

FOR SOMETHING GREATER

Setbacks aren't always meant to be a negative thing but we see it that way because it's standing in the way of the thing we think we want. Setbacks can be a time to reevaluate a situation, a time to refocus, or simple a time to pause before making an irreversible mistake. How we perceive this time is critical. If we are impatient, we may miss the whole point of the setback. Have you ever been running late for work or a meeting and traffic was backed up for miles. But what you didn't know was just a few miles ahead a horrible accident happened. If you had been a few minutes earlier, you could've possibly been involved in that accident. But you're in the car seething about how much time it was taking to reach your destination. Setbacks can work in our favor if we allow it to just be.

#80

ARE YOU LIVING A ONE NOTE LIFE

OR ARE YOU LIVING A SYMPHONY

If you are living a one note life, imagine yourself sitting at a piano striking the same one key over and over again. There is nothing interesting or exciting happening, just status quo. I use to feel like this often. I would wake up in the morning and hop on the preverbal hamster wheel going round and around with no destination in mind. I ran on the wheel all day to accomplish absolutely nothing. It was a pattern I noticed and needed so desperately to change but had no clue where to start. You can live your life as a symphony and play every instrument if only you believe it.

#81

YOU HAVE THE POWER WITHIN

TO DO ANYTHING YOU WANT

Believe in your power, it's real!

ASK YOURSELF A QUESTION: WHAT ARE THE PIVOTAL MOMENTS THAT CHANGED THE TRAJECTORY OF MY LIFE?

My 7 pivotal moments:

1. Listening to inspirational messages from Les Brown and Deepak Chopra in my teens
2. Reading *"The Celestine Prophecy"* in my twenties
3. Moving to Atlanta in my thirties
4. Leaving corporate America in my thirties
5. Working with a group of teenage girls in my thirties
6. Breast cancer diagnosis in my forties
7. Reinventing myself in my forties

THINGS WILL CHANGE

It was in my early twenties I came to know and understand the power of change. I was working in a corporate setting where offices were adorned with motivational framed posters from a company called Successories. The posters were meant to inspire and motivate the company employees. There were depictions of people, places, and things being successful against the odds. My favorite poster hung in my office and it showed a massive wave churning towards the shore and it simply read, "If you don't ride the wave of change you will find yourself underneath it." During that time we were experiencing rolling layoffs throughout the financial services industry. I had several employees, friends, and colleagues who were affected. I would often think about how things were quickly changing around me despite my desire for them to remain the same. Nothing in life is constant but change.

LOOK FOR THE GREATER PURPOSE

Searching for the greater purpose will lead to you living your purpose. The greater purpose is the reason why something is happening.

KEEP MOVING

I'm in my zone now. I can't stop moving even if I wanted to stop moving. There is a fire so fierce inside of me that it keeps me moving in a forward motion. I believe this happens when you are living your purpose. There are times when it seems like you can't take your life to the next level. In those times you may just need to be still. Once the momentum of your life strikes and you get into a rhythm; your life will shift and all you can see is forward. I feel like everything I do is connected to the next thing I will do. It's an amazingly satisfying feeling.

#86

HOLD ON

When you feel like giving up just hold on.
The very thing you want is on the other side of
giving up. I saw a picture of a man who was
digging in a cave for gold. It appeared as though he
had been digging for quite some time. He was
covered in dirt and his clothes were dripping with
sweat. Finally after countless hours and days of
digging, he gave up and walked away. What he
didn't realize was a few more strikes to the wall
would have revealed his golden treasure. No matter
how long you have been striking the preverbal wall,
hold on because the pathway to your hidden
treasures is right on the other side.

AN UNPLANTED SEED HAS POTENTIAL

Potential is worthless if it never gets planted. How many people do you know who have the potential to be great but are too afraid to plant their seeds?

BE STILL

When you have done all you know to do, do nothing. Be still long enough to get answers to the questions you are seeking. In some instances I had no choice but to be still because I was fearful of making another wrong move, so I sat in my stillness. I waited for God to speak to me and guide my steps.

#89

TAKE RESPONSIBILITY FOR YOUR NOW

You can't rewrite your past so don't waste your now trying to rearrange something you have no control over. Instead, create the life you want to see now.

KNOW WHAT YOU WANT

If you don't know what you want then how can you expect to get it? What you want may be right in front of you but you haven't taken the time to be clear about it. I was watching one of my favorite talk shows when the host introduced a guest who thought it was a good idea to have a party where exes are being recycled. Each woman invited to the party was asked to bring their ex-boyfriend. Basically, the women were swapping exes with their friends. Sounded like a good idea at first until the person hosting the party became jealous when she saw her ex-boyfriend talking to her friends. He received so much attention that the host told him certain friends of hers were off limits. He ended up hitting it off with her best friend and it was rather awkward when they all came to the show to talk about their experience. The host admitted she still had feelings for her ex and even said, "I'm not done with him yet." How does someone feel they have the right to hold up someone else's life because they can't make a decision? By the end of the show, the best friend and the host's ex-boyfriend were holding hands. She may not have been done with him but it was obvious he was ready to move on.

SURRENDER

The day I surrendered to the will of God, my life was forever changed. I surrendered and allowed God to have His way with me. I tried it my way for half of a century and did a pretty good job. But I got tired of trying to make things happen on my own. I was exhausted trying to figure out what my next steps should be. Surrendering doesn't mean you have to give up your life, it means you are agreeing to co-create your life with God. He knew exactly what your life would be before you came to this planet. I believe one of our biggest struggles is trying to live a life we weren't meant to live, a life with no purpose. I became teachable for God to give me instructions on what He wanted me to do with my life. He told me to use my life experiences as a lesson plan to transform and have more peace, joy, and happiness.

LOVE YOURSELF

Don't expect others to love you if you don't love yourself.

PAY ATTENTION TO HOW

THINGS MAKE YOU FEEL

Do the people around you decrease or increase your energy? We have all experienced a time when you went into a space and something about it just didn't feel right. We can experience the same thing with people. I am mindful how I feel when I'm around people. I don't like spending my time in situations when I'm uncomfortable. In certain cases you don't have control over if you can vacate the uncomfortable space or not. However, when it comes to my personal life I do have a choice if I want to be around when I'm feeling uncomfortable. Being in touch with how things make you feel can be the conduit for you changing jobs, leaving a purposeless relationship, or anything else you wish to change.

THERE ARE NO GUARANTEES IN LIFE

A woman I knew was fearful to advance her career when offered a job in another department. She wanted so desperately for her current department to create a new position for her to get promoted. She feared the many crisis she would face by taking on the new position. Employees were quitting due to poor working conditions, the worksite had become a virtual revolving door. You have to embrace your fears because things will not always look the way you want. Take the opportunity for growth that will get you closer to the place you want to be. You have to sail the rough seas to get to the stillness of the calm waters. The young woman didn't allow her fears to take over. She accepted the new job and has an opportunity to make the changes she wants to see.

#95

YOUR PARENTS DID THE

BEST THEY KNEW TO DO

We don't come with a manual when we're born. Our parents had their perception of how we should be raised, good bad, or indifferent. Blaming them for what did or didn't happen is futile as we get to a certain point in life. We are responsible for our now and we determine what will happen going forward. Your parents did the best they knew how to do. Stop holding them and yourself hostage for what happened in your childhood. You're an adult so take control of your now and live your purpose.

THE GLASS IS HALF FULL

I knew someone who believed her glass was half empty and has been all of her life. A few short months after making this statement, her life changed tremendously. She applied for a new job and was promoted and her husband was hired by a company who received his resume over a year ago. I wonder if she still feels her glass is half empty.

THE GRASS IS NOT ALWAYS
GREENER ON THE OTHER SIDE

Perhaps if you watered your own grass it would be just as green.

THINK ABOUT WHAT YOU THINK ABOUT

Quiet the mental chatter and listen to your thoughts. If you want to change your life you must first change the way you think. How do you know what you're thinking if you don't think about it? How do you know if you're always thinking negative thoughts if you don't examine what you're thinking about? Negative thinking can become your normal way of thinking but you can combat the mental chatter by challenging negative thinking. If you are having thoughts that are negative and untrue, you should replace them with positive thoughts. If you are having negative thoughts about yourself that are true, then you have to decide what you're going to do about it. You can't change anything in your life until you are aware of what you're thinking.

STEP INTO YOUR GREATNESS

A young man I mentor wrote an amazing play called *"Speechless: The Musical,"* at 19 years old. Speechless debuted in Atlanta at 3 different theatrical venues. He wrote, directed, produced, and starred in the play as well as wrote each song for the soundtrack. I met this young man when he was 15 years old and dealing with some challenging life circumstances. He went to a performing arts high school but by all accounts had no formal training. He knew nothing about writing a play, nothing about how to direct a play or much less write an entire soundtrack of over 20 songs. In my opinion he is a genius. I have never met another human being like him, ever. He wrote Speechless while sitting in his office looking out the window at a group of homeless people. For days he sat at the window imagining their conversations. Being a naturally curious person, he went outside and starting talking with a few of them. He met some pretty interesting people with extraordinary life stories so desperately needing to be told. He thought a play would be a great way to highlight their lives and tell the stories of the voiceless. A few short days later characters began to speak to him and he penned *"Speechless: The Musical. "* In the lyrics to one of the songs on the soundtrack I love the most goes like this "gotta tell this story, gotta share this journey cause there's something you need to know." I believe there is something we all need to share with the world. Be fearless and step into your greatness.

#100

STOP MAKING EXCUSES

Have you ever talked to someone who has an excuse for everything? No matter what you say they always have a retort. Stop making excuses for not living your purpose. People come up with all kind of reasons why they can't start a new business, change jobs, or venture into a new relationship. You will never know the outcome until you stop making excuses and try.

MEDITATE

Sometimes I think about mediation and how powerful I am to be able to stop my mind from thinking any thoughts. What did I just say? I said, "I have the power to stop my mind from thinking during meditation." I know it sounds completely absurd to someone who has never experienced mediation before. I learned how to meditate about 10 years ago at my church, Hillside International Truth Center. Our Founding Minister, Dr. Barbara L. King often spoke about the TM method. It's transcendental meditation. I had no clue what it was because I was new to the concept of meditation. The one thing I know for sure about meditation is it opened the door to my spiritual awakening. I was introduced to a whole new world of my inner self. Three things I have noticed since learning to meditate is a tremendous increase in creativity, mental sharpness, and spiritual insight. It's an enlightening experience and I recommend it to everyone. Most people will either say I don't have time or I can't sit still long enough or I have too many racing thoughts to be able to meditate. This is all the more reason why you should be meditating.

It's a great way to relieve stress and wind down from your day as well as a great way to start your day. All it takes is 20 minutes twice a day. Sometimes I mediate 3 times a day; once in the morning, once at noon, and then again before turning in for the evening. You can start out on a small scale and practice being still for 5 minutes in a quiet space with no interruptions. Social media will certainly be there when you return, it can wait. Once you are comfortable with sitting still for 5 minutes then increase your time. You can incorporate a mantra to focus on while you're sitting still. Anything you find calming to your soul like the sound of a bird or the ocean will suffice. It can even be a word such as peace, joy, or Om. Repeat the word or sound over and over and over and over until you find yourself in a blissful state of nothingness. Like anything else new in your life; it takes time to build your meditation muscle. But once you do, you will find the peaceful place residing within.

ASK YOURSELF A QUESTION:

DO I SHOW COMPASSION?

What does it mean to show compassion towards others? I think it means to see a person. Not just the visual sense of an individual, but to see their pain, to see their struggle or to see them as a human being in need. Often times we are so absorbed with daily distractions that we don't pay attention enough to know we should be showing compassion. I have always had a strong sense of the wounds of humanity. It bothers me to see people hurting and not be able to do something to make it better. One of the reasons I was drawn to the field of psychology is because I get a chance make a difference in the world by helping people.

FOLLOW YOUR INSTINCTS

A friend was on assignment for work in
Myanmar in 2014 before heading to Kiev, Ukraine
a week later. She was sent there to visit with local
officials before heading back to the U.S. She took
some time out to be a tourist while in Myanmar,
seeing some of the temples and monasteries
adorning the country. We did a video chat after her
adventures and it was pretty cool knowing she was
10 and half hours into a new day. She talked about
a dancing toy cat she purchased and the many
beautiful sites she saw. We talked about her
upcoming flight to Ukraine and I wondered if it
would be a good idea for her to go due to the
political unrest they were experiencing. She
assured me everything would be fine because her
higher ups had given the all clear to proceed. I was
thinking her instincts should have kicked in at some
point and she would've abandoned her assignment
and came home, but she didn't.

As she flew from Asia to Europe, I watched
the 24 hour news cycle of the growing unrest in
Kiev where she was scheduled to land. I was
thinking maybe the flights would get cancelled or
maybe she would get a message to come back to the
states early. Neither of those things happened and
she ended up in a hot bed of turmoil. When she
arrived at the hotel she found out some of her

colleagues decided to come back to the states instead of flying into Kiev. The hotel where she was staying was adjacent to Independence Square where most of the unrest was happening. I received an email from her describing how bombs were going off outside as she's checking in to the hotel. It was still daylight outside so they were able to see what was going on. Hotel staff advised them to stay away from doors and windows. At one point they took extra precaution by barricading the front doors. I encouraged her to try to get a flight out as early as possible. The earliest she could leave was 3 days away. She couldn't go to the U.S. Embassy as I suggested because the protestors had blocked the entrance to the embassy.

She stayed in her room which overlooked Independence Square where the protesters had gathered to have a showdown with Ukrainian security forces. Military tanks were visible as she peered through the window to see what was going on. It was surreal for me to see it on the news and to receive live email updates every 2 to 3 minutes. It was in the wee hours of the morning in the U.S. and I had to go to work the next day but I stayed awake because I knew she was afraid. The lobby of her hotel was turned into a makeshift hospital where doctors triaged the wounded. I told my friend to wrap her passport, credit cards, and other important documents in plastic. I then advised her to put them somewhere on her body inside of her clothes just in case she had to exit the hotel quickly.

Molotov cocktails were flying through the air creating devastation wherever they landed. The raging fires they caused didn't care if it were a storefront, an abandoned car, or in the crowd of living breathing human beings. On the day of her departure, my friend was escorted to the hotel basement where the driver awaited to take her to airport under cover of night. She arrived in the United States safely and resigned a few months later. The doctor who once traveled around the world for work now does research and teaches at her favorite university.

BE FEARLESS

It seems like the people I call my friends are either some awesomely fierce chicks or they're just plain crazy. A young friend 15 years my junior and like a little sister to me is one of the most fearless women I know. She surprised us all when announcing she would be moving to Kuwait to teach. Who does this? Many people do. I did it when I joined the Army and was stationed in Germany. Sometimes you just have to follow your instincts and do what feels right. My friend had been teaching for a few years and the opportunity came for her to teach in Kuwait and she took it.

She began to travel once she settled into her new surroundings. In 2013, she went to Turkey in the midst of political uprising of protestors clashing with police in the streets. The only thing I could do was pray because I knew she would go anyway. Her many travels included United Arab Emirates, Sri Lanka, Thailand, Greece, Egypt, South Africa, Oman, Singapore, and Indonesia. I enjoyed seeing the images of her fun adventures from across the globe. She had pictures of herself floating in the Dead Sea, which boarded Israel, the West Bank, and Jordan. Pictures were captured of her volunteering to serve food to monks in Cambodia. My favorite pictures were her with the animals. She rode the backs of elephants and camels, swam with dolphins, hung out with monkeys and sat calmly as a tiger lay perched at her feet. My least favorite was of her holding a huge yellow snake, Brittany Spears style.

The kids she taught adored her and she adored them right back. She would have huge celebrations on holidays and other special days of significance. The kids were delighted to dress in costumes and eat exotic foods from other cultures. They enjoyed many of the American traditional dishes and customs. The kids were 5 to 7 years old and remained in her class for two years. She taught English, Math, Science, Social Studies and Life Skills. A typical school day began around 9:30 am and ended by 1pm. Parents and nannies would usually show up around noon to take the kids home for the day. Her entire Kuwait experience was life changing. She impacted the lives of children who will never forget her. She still does video chats with them and their families on a regular basis since returning to the U.S. last year.

#105

FREEFALL

A short poem…

afraid of pursuing dreams tomorrow

fear of being knocked down by today

haunting sounds of my childhood

growing strong in thorns of anger I pray

fear can no longer paralyze

awakened and transformed I rise

doing what I came here to be

freefall knowing God will catch me

#106

PEACE OF MIND

Another short poem...

my mind was a prisoner of itself

unloving thoughts perched on its shelf

entangled with confusion and chaos

withdrawn and afraid dreams were lost

harassing reminders the absence of love

walls of depression closing in from above

on the brink of insanity a very thin line

now I know peace of mind

#107

ASK YOURSELF A QUESTION: WHAT

ARE MY NATURAL GIFTS AND TALENTS?

Your gifts and your talents are your treasures. It's the key to fulfilling your purpose. How can you begin to identify your natural gifts and talents? Ask yourself what do I do well with little to no effort? What am I willing to do for free? If you want to transform your life to live your purpose, you have to ask yourself some tough questions and be ok with the answers. Life isn't designed to make us feel warm and fuzzy all the time. The best truth is the truth you tell yourself about yourself. We have so many gifts and talents we take for granted that lay dormant within us. We have to bring those gifts and talents to the surface. If you want to have a better life then go within dust off your gifts, polish them up, and nurture them. You could be sitting on a gold mine of ideas but you wouldn't know it because you're so focused on your 9 to 5. Focusing on your 9 to 5 is great if it's tied to your passion. But if it's not and you have more to offer to the world then I suggest you put some energy on other things you do well. We aren't confined to doing just one job for the rest of our lives. Back in the day our parents worked for a company for 20 or 30 years waiting for the precious day to retire. I have no intention of working any job to the day I retire. Our society has shifted so much that most people don't stay on the job long enough to retire anymore. I plan to be one of those people.

#108

REMOVE THE WORDS I CAN'T

FROM YOUR VOCABULARY

How do you know if you can't do it if you haven't tried yet? If you think you can't then you can't. I don't recall when I removed the words I can't from my vocabulary. It was probably early in my search for enlightenment. I would hear motivational speakers talk about choosing your words carefully. I began to examine what it meant and watched how my life turned around when I made a conscious decision to stop saying certain things. Something as simple as the cessation of the words I can't. If Gwyneth Paltrow and Chris Martin can have a conscious uncoupling of their marriage then we certainly can have a conscious uncoupling with the words "I can't."

#109

ADAPT

Adapting is changing to something new when you were comfortable with the old. Well, being comfortable with the old is overrated. Adapting means to accommodate, adjust, and acclimate. All of which we don't do with a smile. We move slowly when we have to do it on our own but what about when you have to adapt and have no choice. You know those times when the company you work for goes through an organizational change. Suddenly you're faced with working for someone you spoke badly about and they know it. What do you do when the person you have been dating for 9 months shows you who they really are instead of being the person you met? Do you stay and adapt or do you run like crazy? I liken adaptation to cycling on an unknown terrain. At certain points along your ride you will have to shift gears to accommodate the rough terrain as it shows up on your path. You will have no choice but to shift gears because if you try to keep riding in one gear you will eventually burn yourself out. Multiple gears are there for a reason, use them. Shift and adapt.

STUCK IN EMOTIONAL IMMATURITY

Immaturity implies a lack of growth. It wasn't until I was well into my forties that I realized I was emotionally immature. By all accounts I was a fully grown functioning adult but my emotions in some areas weren't grown woman like. We react to people based on our life experiences. If a person experiences emotional neglect and abuse then they will react from a place of emotional immaturity. They only know how to relate to others in a certain way because their emotional development is suspended. I am still that little girl looking for emotional nourishment from my mother. This is where I got stuck. You don't move beyond that space until you return to it and heal it. I am now in this moment as I write these words giving myself permission to heal. I love and honor the little girl in me and allow her to flourish and grow. Take a look at the little boy and little girl within you to find out where you need to be healed. The child in you needs to be seen, heard, and validated. One of the most disturbing things I learned about myself was that I was emotionally immature. Here I was standing in a grown woman's body with little girl feelings. I began to think about how I would grow up my feelings. Then I wondered if we were all just grown-ups with little kid's feelings.

#111

COMMIT

I am committed to the journey which lies ahead. I don't know what tomorrow will bring but the unknown doesn't paralyze me with fear. It keeps me excited with the expectancy of something good happening.

#112

WATER THE SEEDS OF GREATNESS

INSIDE OF YOU AND WATCH

YOURSELF COME ALIVE

You have to water your seeds of greatness once you realize they are inside of you. Some people don't believe they possess greatness on the inside. They don't see anything remotely great about themselves but they can see it in others. Your life will blossom once you accept and water those seeds. Watering your seeds of greatness means to believe in yourself, to love yourself, and to motivate yourself. Most importantly giving yourself permission to be authentically who you are.

#113

CHANGE IS GOOD

I had the courage to transform my life into what it is today. I can't imagine being the person I used to be and trying to accomplish the things I'm accomplishing in my life now. I know it would have been virtually impossible with my old way of thinking. My life has changed for the better and I will never be the same. The old was necessary for me to recognize the new.

#114

DON'T RUSH THE LESSONS

You don't have to rush the lessons because they will come as they need to. If you don't get the lessons the first time around you are doomed to repeat them. If you need more lessons in love, they will come. If you need more lessons in how to manage your money, they will come. If you need more lessons in compassion, they will come. If you need more lessons in forgiveness, they will come. Whenever something challenging pops up on my path I automatically wonder what is the lesson here to teach me?

#115

YOU ARE ALWAYS IN MOTION

WHEN LIVING YOUR PURPOSE

Since coming into my own to live my purpose I have noticed an increase in motion. Like most people I am usually busy doing something. But what are we really busy doing? Are we being busy just to say we're busy or are we busy in motion living our purpose? I am busy in motion living my purpose. This means I wake up every morning on a mission. I set the intention for the day and away I go. My mind is focused on all things having to do with my purpose. I breeze through my day with ease taking care of one task at a time. Even when I'm sitting in stillness I'm in motion.

REVELATIONS ARE PLENTIFUL

I was watching Joel Osteen at some point last year and he said "God is going to show you something you have never seen before." Joel has become somewhat of a messenger of God because it seems like many of his messages comes directly from God through Joel to me. Joel's words speak to me at the right place in my life at the right time. God has revealed some things I had never seen before. The funny thing is they were always there I just never noticed them. Many of the revelations have been new things I learned about myself. God reveals things to us when we need to know them. I believe if they were revealed any earlier then we would find a way to mess it up. We receive messages all the time from various sources but we have to be awakened to see them.

REDISCOVER YOUR PASSION

We get so covered in layers that we forget what we are passionate about. We forget about the many things we use to do that brings us joy. Those things can easily be rediscovered again if only we would put some energy on them. I rediscovered my passion for psychology after serving in the military and spending over a decade as a corporate professional. I fell in love with psychol... in high school but was told I would never mak... the field. I had to peel that layer and p... loved. I always had a natural affinity... helping people in whatever way I cou... sounds like a cliché but I really do e... people, especially when they are hu... been told that my words are inspiri... people feel better. Someone once... passionate about and my response... passionate about inspiring others... self."

#118

JUST IN CASE YOU NEED CONFIRMATION

I was inspired to write *"Peeling Back the Layers of Your Life: A Pathway Revealing 365 Hidden Treasures"* as I prepared for a keynote speech at a graduation in December 2015. I thought about my upcoming 50th birthday and what I wanted to do to commemorate the occasion. So many life lessons were learned on my journey and I want to share them with the world. A few days before the speech I was thinking of something I could give to the students. Not only did I want to deliver an impactful speech but I wanted to put something tangible in their hands they could remember. As a general rule for the numerous speaking engagements I've done, I like to leave the audience with three things they need to know. I decided to give each student an envelope with a gold seal on the back enclosed with three gold nuggets. The first three gold nuggets in this book were given to the 2015 GED graduates from The Center for Family Resources, CobbWorks Literacy Council, Paxen Learning Corporation and Youth ASSETS. Their graduation theme was "moving mountains. After my speech, I was greeted by students and parents telling me how inspired they were. Sometimes it's challenging to know if you are going in the right direction. You want assurances that all of your effort is not in vain. These are some of the comments told to me after the speech.

Parent said: "Not only did I hear what you were saying but I could feel it"

Graduate said: "I'm going to remember you forever"

Parent said: "God is all over you"

Pastor said: "You are doing God's work, have you accepted your calling"

Parent said: "Keep touching people's lives"

14 year old boy said: "You have inspired me to follow my dreams"

Council President said: "Just stand next to me while I give the closing remarks because you have such good energy."

Literacy Council Chair: "You were so transparent"

Parents said: "Are the 3 things you need to know just for the graduates or can anyone have them?"

WHEN POTENTIAL MEETS

OPPORTUNITY YOU HAVE GREATNESS

I am at my best when I have the opportunity to show what I can do. The more opportunity knocks the more I will keep answering. The thing about opportunity is you have to be ready to receive it or it will continue to pass you by. Stop looking for opportunity the way you want to see it and just be open to an opportunity. It may be something you never thought of before, something completely out of the purview of your potential. You don't know what you can do until you do it. You limit opportunities when you think they should come packaged in a certain way. Opportunities are limitless and they are all around you. The late great Dr. Wayne Dyer said, "If you change the way you look at things the things you look at will change."

#120

ASK YOURSELF A QUESTION: WHAT HAPPENS WHEN I MAKE UP MY MIND?

Does it take you forever to make a decision or are you a decisive type of person? I'm a decisive type of person. Once I make a decision I stick with it and it doesn't take a lot of time for me to decide. Regardless of how you make decisions, you eventually make them. Once we make the decision to do something we feel pretty comfortable moving forward. So think about if you made a real decision to change your life. You say you want more peace, more joy, and more happiness but why haven't you decided to do it. Decide right now and see what happens. Not just say it but decide. It makes a difference. People say they want to do this or that all the time but in most cases never follow through. I believe something is released inside of you when you finally decide. Your determination is activated and everything within will keep pushing you forward until you see real change happening. You just have to decide.

"Until you are committed, there's hesitancy."
– Oprah Winfrey

BE GRATEFUL

My favorite thought leaders talk about how it makes such a difference in their life to show gratitude. Many of them believe the more gratitude you show the more you receive. The more doesn't necessarily have a monetary value. The more could be more happiness, more peace or more of whatever it is you are seeking. My more is being able to have another day to make a difference. One of my early morning daily rituals is to show gratitude for the new day. I went to hear a young man speak at a meet up group and he talked about how he starts his day in silence showing gratitude. He talked about how his life has increased in many ways by simply focusing on being grateful. He was literally bouncing with excitement when he talked about how grateful he was for everything in his life. He told us how he grew up with very little resources which made him determined to do better for his family. I would recommend shifting your attention more on being grateful instead of focusing on what you don't have. Believe it or not whatever you put your attention on multiplies.

#122

WHAT GOES AROUND COMES AROUND

Karma isn't very nice when she comes back around. Be careful what you put out in the world because it will surely come back. Years ago it seemed like it took karma forever to come back around but she seems to be making her rounds a lot quicker lately. Since living a more conscious life I am extremely mindful of what I put out in the Universe. I put out good energy therefore I receive good energy in return.

TOMORROW IS ANOTHER DAY

Another day for what you may ask, another day to live your best life. Tomorrow isn't promised so you should live your best life every day. If you get a chance at a new day then decide I will live my best life. If you don't know what your best life looks like, take some time to think about what makes you happy. If you don't know what makes you happy then think about what it will take to make you happy and what you are willing to do to be happy. You have to do something because it's not going to happen on its own. So often we can easily articulate what we don't want but have no clue about what we do want. The beauty in life is you have the answers right in front of you if only you would look to see what's there.

#124

CULTIVATE RELATIONSHIPS

I spent many years as corporate professional cultivating relationships with my clients as a Relationship Manager. I knew in order to retain their business I had to nurture the relationship. I had to put in some time understanding their business and keep the lines of communication open. Much like what you should do to maintain any other type of relationship. It seems like people don't really value cultivating relationships with one another. Relationships appear to be disposable. We don't even relate to each other like we use to. Instead of picking up a phone to see how a person is doing, we would rather send a text or scroll through a time line on social media to get a recent update. I understand times have changed but any relationship worth having is worth cultivating. When you connect on a deeper level you will find that your relationships are more fulfilling. You're probably thinking if I go deeper in my relationships I may get hurt. The risk of being hurt is an absolute possibility. I'm not saying to connect deeper with everyone you meet because everyone you meet isn't worthy of your depth. What I am saying is, when you meet someone and organically connect take the risk to go deeper.

#125

BELIEVE IN YOURSELF

Believing in yourself isn't something you automatically do when you pop out of the womb. It's hard to believe in yourself when the people around you don't believe in you. Many of the young people I have encountered don't have anyone to teach them to believe in themselves. It's so easy to give up when you don't believe in yourself.

#126

BIRDS DO SING IN THE RAIN

I often wondered if birds sing in the rain. They actually do sing in the rain. I was sitting in my room on a rainy Saturday afternoon. I opened the window to take in the smell of the rain when much to my surprise the birds were singing. They also sing in the winter when it's 30 degrees outside. If a bird can still sing in 30 degree weather, what in the world do we have to complain about?

DON'T GIVE UP

     I often tell young people that giving up isn't an option so try something else. Even if you take smaller steps or if it takes you twice as long, keep moving and don't give up. Giving up is easy, it takes no effort and it's predictable.

ALLOW GOD TO HAVE

HIS WAY WITH YOU

God wants the absolute best for us. When I realized this simple truth, I surrendered and allowed Him to have his way with me. It's not like I didn't know this before but as I began to strengthen my relationship with Him it became more evident. He taught me that in order for me to help others to transform, I first had to be transformed. I feel like a weight has been lifted off of my shoulders because I'm not doing this life thing alone. His presence is always around me, guiding me every step of the way. I no longer live for what I want for my life. I live for what God wants for my life. I have a pretty wild imagination but what He wants for my life far exceeds anything I can ever imagine. I want what God wants for my life.

GIVE YOURSELF TIME TO GROW

INTO WHO YOU ARE GOING TO BE

I had to grow into being positive, not just my words but my actions. I dealt with depression just like millions of people do. I struggled with believing in myself. In our world of immediate gratification, there is no app that you can swipe left or right to achieve instant transformation. We have way too much baggage to think we can swipe it away overnight. You have to do the work yourself and understand it will take some time to adjust. A friend gave a great analogy about transformation. She asked "How do you eat an elephant?" I look perplexed and horrified at the thought of eating an elephant and didn't know how to respond. She then said, "One piece at a time." Transformation occurs the same way, one piece at a time.

IDENTIFY MULTIPLE STREAMS OF

INCOME DOING WHAT YOU LOVE

I was teaching a class and some of the students were complaining about their salary. My response, "You knew what you signed up for so your salary shouldn't be a surprise." If you are unhappy with your current salary then use your gifts to make money now. Stop depending on a raise at work that may never come. There are plenty of other things you can do to generate income. I don't mean picking up a part-time job to supplement your income, although sometimes it may be required in the interim. What I'm really saying is when you identify multiple streams of income by using your gifts; it should be something in alignment with your purpose. Take inventory of what you do well and find a way to make money doing it. I was watching Shark Tank one lazy Friday evening after work and Daymond John the founder of FUBU said, "He makes money while he sleeps." How great is it to be able to say while I was asleep last night, I was making money. Especially if you're doing something you love.

#131

CHALLENGE YOURSELF

If you walk into a room and you're the smartest person in the room then you're in the wrong room. One thing I know about myself is if I'm not being challenged then I'm bored. I'm not saying I have to constantly be put in a position where I'm faced with challenging situations. My definition of challenging oneself is pushing beyond the limits of where I am to reach the next level of my greatness. For too many years I was operating at the lowest level of my being. I knew I was capable of more but I didn't push for it. We are all capable of doing more so why not just do more instead of thinking we can.

#132

ATTENTION TOXIC PEOPLE,

PLEASE TAKE TWO STEPS TO

THE LEFT SO I CAN PASS YOU BY

Take inventory of the people you have sitting in the front row of your life. Some of them don't belong there and probably snuck in when you weren't paying attention. Others you may have allowed in because you didn't want to be alone. Right now, I declare all toxic people to take two steps to the left so my readers can pass you by.

LIFE WILL TEST YOU

What do you do when life tests you while in pursuit of your dreams? Do you give up on your dream and go back to what was comfortable? Or do you keep pushing until you see a breakthrough. All too often when life tests people it stops them dead in their tracks. I see tests as something to strengthen my resolve. It builds my character and gives me the enthusiasm I need to keep moving forward regardless of the circumstances. I have learned that life's tests are temporary and won't last forever.

YOUNG PEOPLE NEED OUR SUPPORT

I was sitting at work on a conference call when I received an email from a colleague who was also on the call. The email stated she received a call from a local non-profit organization needing their support. My colleague didn't really provide me with the particular needs of the organization, just a flyer advertising an overnight youth lock-in. I decided to reach out to the founder to offer my services as a speaker. Much to my surprise, I received a quick response saying she would love to have me a part of the event and that her PR team would be in contact. One thing led to another and I participated in the Gocha Illumination Foundation Youth Lock-In inaugural event held at the Center of Hope this year. I always wanted to participate in this type of event but something always seemed to come up, perhaps it just wasn't the right time.

Imagine being locked in a facility with over 40 teenage girls. I couldn't think of anywhere else I would rather be on a Friday night than to be in a position to inspire young minds. It was great to see the young ladies so eager for what the night had in store for them. The theme of the event focused on leadership, self-esteem, and problem solving. The welcome kickoff rally featured encouraging words from founder Gocha Hawkins, Atlanta City Councilman Kwanzaa Hall, Kandi Burruss, and others who came together to get the girls ready for their mentoring sessions. The girls enjoyed a mini concert by R&B group Glamour and had plenty of food to eat throughout the night and well into the morning hours. Gocha's amazing team of stylists gave the girls manicures, haircuts, and press n'curl hairstyles.

I had the great pleasure of facilitating four leadership sessions. We started the sessions around 9:30 pm and ended about 1:30 am. The girls were engaged as they talked about the important traits of what a leader should possess. They listed things like; honest, creative, fearless, open-minded, role model, confident, responsible, inspirational, and hard working. One of the most important traits of a leader said by all four groups is that a leader should have a vision. One of the girls said, "Who wants to follow someone with no vision?" These young ladies were very sharp and displayed many of the traits of a leader themselves. After some discussion about leadership, the girls created vision boards and talked about their hopes and dreams. I reminded them to keep their vision board in a place where they can see it every day.

After the sessions were done the girls started to settle down a bit to watch movies, play games, and eat more food. I shifted from being a speaker to being a chaperone. The girls laughed and talked until about 4am. It was a great experience to be a part of an organization that brought together a team of people to show their support. All of the mentor speakers spread their words of wisdom and encouragement to these phenomenal young ladies. Their lives will be forever changed and mine will be too. I gave the girls 3 gold nuggets which read: You are beautiful the way you are, commit yourself to excellence, and elevate your thinking.

IT'S TIME TO SHARE YOUR

GIFTS WITH THE WORLD

One of the reasons I wrote this book is because it was time for me to share my gifts with the world. I have been sharing my wisdom and knowledge for years with any and everyone who would listen. Something inside kept nudging me to do it on a larger platform. I would jokingly tell people I'm giving you this information for free now but one day you will pay a lot of money to come hear me speak. I can recall sitting at a conference listening to speakers and thinking to myself, I can do that. My mind would drift off on the different topics I would address. I began to visualize what I would be wearing and how I would move around the room to engage with my audience. My gifts are beginning to move from everyday conversations with friends and co-workers to wider audiences. I'm receiving calls and emails more frequently to speak at conferences and to partner with individuals who are seeking inspiration and empowerment. One of my greatest passions is to spread messages of hope, love, and inspiration.

#136

YOU ARE NEVER TOO BUSY

People are always saying they are too busy to do this, that or the other. If it's important you will make time. You have to ask yourself am I being effective. Just because you're busy doesn't mean you're being effective or productive for that matter.

DON'T LET NOBODY REARRANGE YOU

People will try it. They want to try and rearrange you to be more suitable in their eyes. Sometimes you are simply a reflection and they don't want to see the truth of who they really are. You make them uncomfortable so they try to change you. Other people's discomfort of who I am is not my concern.

#138

PRACTICE MINDFULNESS

Practicing mindfulness isn't some mystical abstract concept only reserved for Buddhist monks. It's something we all can do that will make a difference in our lives. Mindfulness is simply placing your attention on intention. The things we place our attention on increases, the things we don't place our attention on decreases. Practicing mindfulness is being consciously aware of what's happening. When you are distracted by electronic devices, you are not in a state of mindfulness. The need to constantly check your social media page to see who liked your latest selfie; you are not in a state of mindfulness. If you are out to dinner with someone and both of you are looking down at your smartphones instead of talking, you are not in a state of mindfulness. We can connect to mindfulness simply by shifting our attention back to what's important.

#139

GOD'S GOT IT

Get out of the way because He doesn't need your help. However, He does need you to act when called upon. Co-creating your life with God means He guides and you follow. Not just sometimes or when you feel like it but all the time.

#140

WATCH YOUR CHILDREN

I jokingly call myself the "child whisperer" because I feel like I was put here to watch over them and in some way make their lives better. It just seems like kids are always drawn to me and me to them. I think they are the greatest. I was in a retail store when I noticed a little boy standing by himself with no parent in sight. I did what I always do which is to stand by to see if a parent would eventually show up. After a few minutes, I walked over to the child but keeping in mind to maintain my distance. I asked the little boy where was his mommy. He looked at me, shrugged his shoulders and said, "I don't know." I asked him what was mommy's name and he said, "Mommy." He then ran over to me and grabbed me around my leg. I stood there in the middle of the store with this kid clinging on to me for dear life. He was just a little guy, maybe 4 or 5 years old. Security was called and before they arrived, the mother showed up. She screamed at the boy saying, "Why did you leave me?" I'm sure the kid was probably thinking the same thing. I'm not a parent but the safety of children is extremely important to me. Unfortunately, we live in a world where terrible things happen to children every day. I see firsthand what can happen to a child who isn't properly supervised. I am a Certified Instructor and Chairperson on the Georgia Statewide Human

Trafficking Task Force. I often encounter people who think human trafficking and sexual abuse of children really doesn't happen. But it does and probably more frequently than one can imagine. It can happen to any child at any time. Predators are simply waiting for the right opportunity to take advantage of a child.

#141

DON'T BRING YOUR DAY HOME

I leave work at work and I leave home at
home. As soon as I get home, I take a hot shower to
wash away any residual work stuff that may be
hanging around. My home is my sanctuary, my
place of peace, and rest. For the most part I do a
good job at maintaining separation between work
life and home life. It's not always an easy thing to
do but you have to practice having a balanced life.

#142

SAVE YOUR MONEY

I can hear my mother's voice in my head as I type these words.

#143

MY LIFE IS A SCAVENGER HUNT

Your whole life will open up the day you rediscover why you were born. You will begin to experience things you have never experienced before. Your life path changes and you are being led by an energy of living your purpose. I was telling a friend I'm feeling as though the Universe is playing a game of hide and go seek with me. I'm beginning to see things that were once hidden, but have been in plain view for years. It wasn't until I allowed myself to fully surrender and co-create my life with God that I was able to see the hidden treasures laid before me. I feel like a little kid on a scavenger hunt looking for the next clue. Each thing I find leads me to the next step I should take on my life path. It's a surreal feeling to be led in such an intentional way.

The week after my 50th birthday a gold imprint of my hand came into my awareness. It was created in preschool when I was 5 years old. For years it sat under my nightstand without me hardly ever noticing it. My father had it on his dresser when I was a kid and would place his keys and loose change on it when he came home from work. Since walking on a life path of purpose I am able to see things I never saw before. There isn't a day that goes by that I don't hear the word gold or see something gold. On a metaphysical level the color gold is associated with enlightenment, wisdom, and a deep understanding of self.

I was listening to a friend being interviewed about a salon she opened in midtown Atlanta last year called Gocha Salon. The interviewer asked her how was she able to do it. Gocha responded, "Everything I touch turns to gold." When I heard her say it I looked over at my gold hand print and smiled. A few weeks later I was a speaker at her foundation's inaugural all girl youth-lock in event. When I walked into the room where I would be speaking there were handprints on the wall made by little children. I brought my handprint so I could show the girls how magical life can be and to look for its hidden treasures. I feel like my gold hand print is a reminder of the imprint I make on the lives of others.

IT'S NEVER TOO LATE

Here I am at 50 years old publishing my first book. My second and third one will be coming out shortly thereafter. I use to think I was a late bloomer until I figured out that everything happens when it should. Right timing is the key. The things we want in life may not happen when we want. It no longer discourages me because I know either it's not time or God has something better coming. I would rather wait on my something better than to settle. It's never too late to follow your dreams. You can start today by shifting the way you see your life. Dig a little deeper to find out what you're supposed to be doing and get busy doing it. Honor your life by doing something meaningful.

#145

EMBRACE MONDAYS

Today is Monday and I always get the most interesting responses whenever I ask someone how they are doing on a Monday. The responses range from "Uh, it's Monday" to "I'm doing okay for a Monday." What is that about? On Friday the responses are dramatically different. I see my co-workers practically doing the moonwalk in the lobby on the way to their cars. I find myself getting caught up in the magic of Fridays. I joke with my peers that they will see me doing donuts in the parking lot as I burn rubber leaving the building. So why is it so difficult to have the same kind of joy on a Monday?

#146

GET OUT OF YOUR WAY

Sometimes we can be our own worst enemy with negative thinking. We don't have to worry about others trying to bring us down because we do a good job all on our own. I had to tell myself to get out the way to make room for something good to happen in my life. How could I possibly think my life would get better by continuing to do things the same way? If we think we can continue to do things the same way and expect change to happen then we are mistaken. You have to be a representative of the change you want to see in your life and the world at large.

#147

ASK YOURSELF A QUESTION:

WHERE IS THE PATH I'M ON TAKING ME?

It's challenging to know if you're on the right path. It's challenging to even know what the right path is for your life. There are signs all around us telling us if we are going in the right direction. Life is speaking to us all the time. There isn't a week that goes by that I don't get a nod along the way from the Universe encouraging me to continue. I was on a path a few years ago that was taking me farther away from my dream. I had to get clear about my purpose for being on this planet. I was pursuing a career which had absolutely nothing to do with my purpose. It wasn't until I was clear about my purpose that I was able to change direction. I know without a doubt the path I'm on is taking me closer to my dreams.

.

#148

BE RECEPTIVE

To be receptive is to be flexible, approachable, accessible, open minded, and amenable. I use to be the exact opposite; I was rigid, unapproachable, closed off, and surrounded by walls as tall as the Great Wall of China. How did I change it? I just got sick and tired of being that way. When you get to a point where you're tired of your own nonsense, you will change. Studying psychology really helped me to understand myself on a deeper level. I begin to ask myself why did act a certain way or why did I respond in a certain way? I genuinely wanted to know and I knew the only person who could answer those questions was me.

CONSISTENT POSITVE THOUGHTS

AND ACTIONS ATTRACTS SUCCESS

If you take the same action then you will get the same reaction. If you take different action then you will attract something different. The point is you have to take action and do it consistently. Your thinking will determine what you attract into your life, be it positive or negative. Take a look at your life right now to see what you have attracted. Your thoughts and actions a few months ago or even a few years ago is what you have attracted into your life now. Positive thought and action amplifies the momentum of attracting success.

GUARD YOUR INNER SANCTUARY

I am acutely aware that God wants me to shine my light on the darkness. He wants me to bring my light where no light dwells. However, with that being said; I know I need to guard my inner sanctuary as I shine my light because negativity abounds. I was standing next to a woman at the checkout counter and she was telling the cashier she was having a crappy day. She went on and on about how bad her day was, in my summation her complaints didn't amount to anything major. No family member died, the kids were safe, and no major life catastrophe was happening so I didn't get it. I took a few steps backwards to move away from her because the negative energy was so strong. I had to put some space between us to preserve my inner sanctuary.

#151

BE CLEAR

Understanding how your dreams are connected to your life purpose is very important. A lot of times we pursue dreams without really understanding why we are doing it. We pursue dreams because we think it will bring financial freedom. We pursue dreams because someone may have told us it was a good idea. We pursue dreams because someone told us we can't do it. Whatever your reason for pursuing your dreams, have some clarity. I wrote down 3 questions when I began writing my first book in 2002. First, I wanted to know why I was writing the book. Second I needed to know what I wanted to say. Lastly, I wanted to know how the book would benefit my readers. The answer to all of the questions was one in the same and directly connected with my life purpose.

#152

ASK YOURSELF A QUESTION:

WHAT KIND OF FRIEND AM I?

In order to have a friend you have to be a friend. What type of qualities do you look for in a friendship? Everything you are looking for you should reflect. If you want a friend who is kind then you should be kind, if you want a friend who is caring then you too should be caring. People befriend each other for various reasons, some for actual friendship and others strictly for networking purposes. To me, networking has nothing to do with friendship. It's not an authentic feeling when people want to be close because they think you can do something for them. I have no issues with helping people but let's not call it a friendship. Most times people hang around long enough to get what they want then they are on to the next. Friendship for me is about mutual respect, reciprocity, and a shared interest in wanting to get to know each other. Friendship is something I don't take lightly.

FIND YOURSELF HIDDEN

DEEP WITH YOURSELF

If you want to know who you are take a journey inside of yourself. All things are hidden until revealed. All things are asleep until awakened. States of consciousness are stagnant until evolved. There is a life inside of us that we fear. We fear getting to the core of ourselves.

A young black man sitting in solitary confinement began to realize there was something happening on the inside of him. The something happening inside of him was change. His story was no different than any other young black male growing up in an inner city neighborhood. His story was no different than the countless young men I have worked with during my tenure in the criminal justice system. He found himself serving almost 20 years in prison for killing a man during a drug deal gone wrong. He once was a young black man living the "thug life." He was surrounded by peers who banded together to form a family to replace the one they didn't have at home. Inside they were all broken. Not broken because there was something wrong with them. Broken because their lives were filled with broken dreams and broken promises.

As the young man sat in solitary confinement, he asked himself how he went from being an honor roll student to sitting in solitary confinement. This is a very good question because if he never asked himself the question he would never have found the answer. If you don't know how to begin your journey within to find your truth, simply ask yourself the question, "Who am I?" Whatever questions you seek the truth about, ask it. It may seem silly to ask yourself a question because if you knew the answer you wouldn't have to ask the question. The young man sitting in solitary confinement had plenty of time to ask questions and listen for his truth. He probably didn't like what he heard but it was his truth.

GET PLENTY OF REST

I was speaking to someone who asked my advice on what she should do in a particular situation. She explained how she had been working overtime for the last month and had taken a short break to get some rest. The time was coming up for her to resume working overtime again but she felt she needed a little more time to rest. She asked me what she should do. I gave her the look as if to say "You already know the answer to this question." I smiled and she said, "I think I need to take more time to rest." I told her she had made a great choice. I have learned not to do more than my body is willing to do because it will shut down. I always yield to my body's command.

I was speaking to a professor the prior day at an advisory board meeting and she was talking about how tired she had been because she was doing too much. She happily went home to announce to her family that she wasn't cooking and everyone needed to figure out their meal plan for the week. Her husband stepped in and made sure everyone was taken care of for the week. He watched her on countless nights staying up until 1am to complete a task then up again at 5am to start a new day. He would always encourage her to leave it for another day but she insisted on getting it done. It wasn't until her failure to get rest made her sick is when she recognized she needed to do something different. Sometimes others can see what we can't and it's not until we recognize it that change will happen. In reality, that one task you just have to finish before you go to get bed just turns into another task, then another task, and another. Find a stopping place then go to bed at a reasonable hour.

I heard someone say he only gets about 4 hours of sleep a night. This guy has multiple things going on simultaneously and I don't see how he can sustain his schedule. He believes in this philosophy so much that he encouraged others to do the same thing while in pursuit of their dreams. There was a time when I actually believed it and was doing this while I was in graduate school. Not because he encouraged me to do it but because I was doing it long before I heard him say it. I use to come home after working 8 or more hours, sit down to have dinner then immediately hit the books. I would study until midnight then take a shower, guzzle down an energy drink, then study a few more hours. Some nights I wouldn't even go to sleep. On other occasions I would change up my routine a bit and throw in a nap here and there. It wasn't until I was diagnosed with breast cancer that my entire routine changed. I look back at it now and wonder what I was thinking. I was doing way too much.

DO NOTHING

One of my favorite things to do is NOTHING! I enjoy lounging around knowing I don't have anything I have to do in that moment. Sometimes I feel a twinge of guilt because I feel like I should be doing something. Then the thought quickly dissipates into the nothingness from whence it came.

FAILURE IS NOT THE END OF THE WORLD

I don't look at anything in my life as a failure. I look at it as an opportunity to get better.

EXPRESS YOURSELF

Self-expression can be challenging especially if you're not accustomed to doing it. In many spaces in our society, self-expression is frowned upon if the way you express goes against what's "normal." I've always wanted to meet the people who set the standard for what is and isn't normal. Some people struggle so much just to fit in and to feel accepted. People repress who they really are because they don't want to feel the pain of rejection. I struggled with this for many years of my life. It wasn't that I was concerned about what others thought because I could care less about what the outside world thought. It was inside of my own home where I didn't feel safe to express myself. Self-expression in my house was a no no. I lived in a "this is the rule and you follow it" environment, which is ok because kids need to understand boundaries. But kids also need to able to grow into who they were naturally created to be. We are creative beings with a multitude of ways of expressing the unique qualities we possess. My self-expression in early adulthood was awkward, immature, and childlike at times because I didn't have much practice in my early years. Sometimes even now it remains a struggle in certain situations.

WHAT YOU THINK

ABOUT YOU WILL ATTRACT

You will notice a common theme of this particular gold nugget being repeated throughout the book. We learn through repetition so I felt it was important to repeat it in different ways. My intention is for this one to really sink in and for you to get it. The idea that your thoughts create your life is a hard concept to swallow if you're not familiar with the philosophy of New Thought. I can tell you that when I was dwelling in the darkest of negative thinking, my life was a representation of my thoughts. It was interesting because I was reading the self-help books and listening to endless hours of inspiration on public television, still thinking the same old thoughts. Even though I didn't see an outward display of this new information having an affect on me, my subconscious was being profoundly impacted. I kept reading and listening until a shift happened and I started to think differently. When I started to think differently a whole new world opened up and my life began to represent my thoughts in a positive way. Life transformation occurs over time; don't give up feeding yourself positive messages because eventually you will feel the shift.

Here are a few key words as it relates to New Thought: positive thinking, consciousness, abundant life, higher thinking, omnipotence, law of attraction, healing, metaphysical, personal power, purpose, intention, co-creation, visualization, transformation, divine intelligence, spiritual awareness, awakened life, and elevation. This isn't a comprehensive list but it's a good place to start if you want to begin to open your mental space to gain new insight about yourself.

#159

YOU CAN'T PLEASE EVERYONE

So stop trying. I have learned the more you do to try to please others, the more they want you to do. They will never be satisfied and it will never be enough. Focus on what pleases you and the rest will work itself out.

STOP THINKING ABOUT ALL THE BAD THINGS YOU ARE AND START THINKING ABOUT ALL THE GOOD THINGS YOU ARE

It's so easy to think about all the bad things about ourselves. Try something new and think only about the good things you are. If you can't think of any good things about yourself then start by making a list of good things you would like to be. Look at that list every day and recite "I AM" in front of each of the good things on the list for 21 days. I use 21 days as a threshold because it takes 21 days to change a habit. Begin today by changing the habit of negative self-thinking.

INSPIRATION IS IN THE AIR

Creativity and ideas are all around us hidden in plain sight. We are often too distracted and too unaware to see it for ourselves. People often wonder how I stay inspired. It's pretty simple because I make it a habit of seeking inspiration daily.

THERE ARE NO COINCIDENCES

Everything happens as it should. I am in the right place at the right time at all times.

VOLUNTEER

A volunteer opportunity led me to the pathway to my purpose. People often scoff at the idea of volunteering because they feel they should receive some type of monetary compensation. College students approach me all the time about how to break into their industry of interest and my first response is to become a volunteer. What better way to learn more about the organization and make connections with key decision makers. A woman came up to me after a speaking engagement to ask how her son could become employed with my agency. She stated he recently graduated and applied for a position but hadn't heard anything yet. I asked if her son had any experience working with young people in detention or any other setting. She said he didn't have any experience working with kids at all. I graciously offered information about our volunteer services program in order for him to get some experience. She looked at me and said, "I always thought it was who you know and not what you know." I thought to myself, I don't know you or your son which means I can't make any recommendations for employment on his behalf. For me, the greatest thing about volunteering is you get to help people. In my opinion helping others should be something we do automatically without hesitation. I started volunteering as a teen and found it to be rewarding to know I am making a difference in someone else's life.

CHANGE YOUR THOUGHTS

CHANGE YOUR LIFE

You have the power within you to change your life simply by changing the way you think. You can master your thoughts by controlling what you think about.

KNOW WHEN IT'S TIME TO GO

There is truth in the words season, reason, and lifetime. I saw the writing on the wall often throughout my life time when it was time to make the next move. Whether it be a career, a relationship or any other situation, there are signs along the way letting you know when it's time to go. Take heed and get moving. If you don't life will happen and make the change for you. The signs will start out as a gentle nudge, you will ignore it. Then you get another gentle nudge and you will ignore it several more times. All of sudden the gentle nudge will turn into a deliberate push. The deliberate push will be life happening without your participation. Don't be mad about it because you had several warnings signs to alert you to this seemingly sudden change. Fear will keep us in situations we probably shouldn't be in. Fear gives us a false sense of security because we think if we stay in the situation we know what to expect.

#166

I DESERVE IT

Whatever your definition of it is, you deserve to have it. Once you come to your own understanding of what you deserve, you open up the flood gates to receive your good.

YOU ARE THE SOURCE

TO YOUR OWN HAPPINESS

Looking outside of yourself for happiness will leave you feeling empty and unfulfilled. Real happiness comes from within. Build your sanctuary of happiness from the inside out.

#168

I CAN

Tell yourself all of the reasons why you can
instead of all the reasons why you can't.

MISTAKES ARE AN

OPPORTUNITY FOR GROWTH

There is something on social media called throwback Thursday where people post pictures of themselves form the "good old days." I post a picture every now and then of myself during happier times in my life. Like most people we want to remember the good times. I posted a quote on social media that read, "Throwback Thursday is reminiscing about the good times and not focusing on the bad times. Personal growth is always the goal." It's nice to look back at the good old days. Unfortunately, those good times are mixed in with the bad times and people get hung up on the bad times and can't move forward. They worry about their past mistakes instead of focusing on the goodness of now. Mistakes comes about to help us grow. How do we know what we are made of if we don't make mistakes and learn from them?

#170

IT'S TEMPORARY

When you find yourself going through a rough time it's challenging to think positive thoughts. I want you to have comfort in knowing the rough times are temporary and you will make it through to the other side. When I was diagnosed with breast cancer in 2012, I kept saying to my mom that I can't wait to get to the other side. I knew what I was going through was temporary and I would live through it to tell my story. Sometimes rough times come about so we can tell our story with the hopes it will help someone else.

#171

DON'T WORRY ABOUT
WHAT PEOPLE THINK OF YOU

People are going to think what they want about you so why concern yourself.

#172

ASK YOURSELF A QUESTION: WHAT

DID I LEARN FROM MY STRUGGLES?

I did a workshop with a group of girls
called, "What's Behind Your Mask?" The girls
traced their hands on construction paper and put
them together to make a mask. They decorated the
front of them with colorful markers and glitter. I
asked them to write words on the front of their
masks how they want the world to see them. Some
girls wrote strength, powerful, smart, beauty,
kindness, and honest. On the back of their masks I
asked the girls to write down words about
themselves they don't want the world to see. They
wrote down the words criminal, liar, bad person,
abused, neglected, and struggle. When I saw the
word struggle I immediately wondered what this
young lady was referring to. What could have
happened in her short life time for the word struggle
to be something she doesn't want the world to see?
It then made me wonder if she learned anything
from her struggles.

#173

SAY A KIND WORD

It takes little to no effort to say something kind to another. Use your words to elevate someone instead of using your words for the opposite. Believe it or not, you become elevated when you use your words for good.

#174

GO INSIDE AND DISCOVER

THE BEAUTY WITHIN

Your outer beauty can fade but your inner
beauty radiates and shines through for the world to
see. Have you ever met someone who was
absolutely drop dead gorgeous but had a crappy
personality? Just because you look good on the
outside doesn't mean you are reflecting the same on
the inside. I take pride in being consistent, so it's
important for my outer beauty to be a reflection of
my inner beauty. The light from your inner beauty
allows you to be just as beautiful on the outside.
We should spend just as much energy primping and
pruning the inner self as much as we do the outer. I
tell my young ladies all the time to have something
more to offer than just your pretty face.

QUIET YOUR INNER CRITIC

We get enough criticism from the world around us so why do we insist on doing it to ourselves. Being your own worst critic is of no benefit to your well-being. It's not motivating, it's not empowering but it is unnecessary. Turn down the volume on your inner critic and one day when you're not paying attention, your inner critic will be gone.

YOU ALREADY KNOW WHAT TO DO

I went to the grocery store to get some stash to hold me over for a few days because the impending winter storm threatened sleet, snow, and icy roads in Atlanta. It sounds funny to think about this happening in Georgia but it can get pretty ugly if you're not prepared. As I was piling my groceries on the conveyor belt, the cashier asked if I was prepared for the upcoming storm. I smiled and nodded yes. He grew up in South Florida just as I did. He told me a story of how his grandpa taught him how to make oatmeal using sterno. He hated oatmeal but ate it anyway. The young man went on to say how we could pretty much get by on what we already have in our pantry. He was probably right, but there is something about hearing a storm is coming that makes you run out and buy a little bit more just in case. This was always the norm when I lived in Florida and hurricane season rolled around. People would load up on wood or steel panels to cover their windows. Then run over to buy the food essentials their family needed. Water, bread, peanut butter, eggs, milk, and cereal were always the first items to fly off the shelf. Whether you are preparing for a hurricane, a massive snow fall or storms of life, there is something within you that already knows what to do.

#177

GET TO KNOW YOURSELF

We go to great lengths to get to know other people. We spend time talking to them, wanting to know everything that ever happen to them since birth. But we don't make the same effort in getting to know ourselves. Getting to know ourselves leads us to understanding our purpose for being on this planet. Knowing our purpose leads us to more joy, more peace, and more happiness. We live a more fulfilling life when we are living our purpose. But you can only do that by getting to know yourself. Learning about yourself is no different than learning anything else you want to know about. Before you enter a classroom you may know a little something about the subject but by end of the semester you have become an expert in the subject. I heard a young man speak at a meet up group and he talked about how he knew more about celebrities than he knew about himself. He eventually figured out knowing such details about others had absolutely nothing to do with his purpose. Get to know yourself, you might actually find out you like yourself.

THINK

We have lost the art of thinking. I call thinking an art because philosophers like, Socrates, Aristotle and others sat around all day just thinking. I've decided that I'm going to call myself a philosopher because to be a philosopher means you study ideas about knowledge, truth, and the meaning of life. We have lost this precious art because we allow our smartphones to do the thinking for us. I'm noticing an increasing number of gadgets designed to encourage us to think less. If we're thinking less then what's happening to the gray matter between ours ears. Kids are completing homework on computers, they pull up search engines online and with a few clicks they have the answers to anything they want to know. Don't get me wrong, I believe in progress and the fact that technology plays an integral role in our everyday lives. It just seems we don't have to think as much as we use to. If you didn't know how to spell a word our parents would always say go look it up. Thinking back on that now, how did they expect us to look up the word if we didn't know how to spell it in the first place? Somehow we made it work and learned how to spell. I was laughing with a friend about the old days when we had to use encyclopedias to help us write book reports as kids. I remember my parents purchased a set of encyclopedias from a struggling college student. I guess the encyclopedia was no different than having a search engine handy, it just took longer. Information has to come from somewhere but why not use your brain to facilitate the process.

FORGIVE

Forgiveness is not for the other person as much as it is for you.   If you are unforgiving then how do you expect to be forgiven? You are walking around carrying the poison of unforgiveness while the other person is completely oblivious. You can forgive someone and still be mindful of what was done. Don't dwell on it because God will give you beauty for your ashes and before you know it restoration has taken its place.

#180

LAUGH

I make it my goal to laugh at something every single day throughout the day. I believe when you make something your intention it will happen. If you seek laughter then laughter is what you will find. The very nature of my job is so serious and I hear such tragic stories one couldn't begin to imagine. I have to counteract the tragedy with laughter. A good belly laugh just makes you feel good all over. You release tension and stress when you laugh. I'm sure it probably does something to the chemicals in your brain to make you feel warm and fuzzy. I advise everyone to make it a priority to seek laughter daily.

#181

SIMPLIFY YOUR LIFE

Life is complex enough without us introducing anything else into the mix. I am always looking at ways to simplify my life. You never know what life brings so for me, I enjoy the luxury of simplicity. I look at shows on the home network channel and I see a growing trend of people moving into small portable houses. I think it's a great way to release things that no longer serve you. We are so focused on hanging on to stuff that when circumstances happen to release them before we are ready, we are left devastated. Someone reading this is sitting on the fence trying to decide if they should release something or not. Just by the mere fact you are sitting on the fence is an indication you should release it. You can't fly if you're being held down by baggage.

#182

WAKE UP WITH EXPECTANCY

Generally, I think we get exactly what we expect in life. Realistically speaking that is. We spend so much time waiting for something to happen instead of expecting it to happen. My life has been so different since deciding to wake up expecting something good to happen. Every day something good does happen. My day is much lighter because I don't place emphasis on things that aren't important. For the last 6 months I have focused my attention on this book. I eat, sleep, and breathe this book until the day of publication. I feel like something inside of me has its foot on the gas and I'm riding at a hundred miles an hour. I've never been this driven about anything in my life before. It's a new way of living; it's a new way of being. I wish more people can feel what I feel right now.

#183

EVERY NEW DAY IS FILLED

WITH POSSIBILITIES

I enjoy the dawning of a new day because it brings with it the possibilities of an unfulfilled yesterday.

SEEK TRUTH

Not what you want to see but the truth. The most important truth to seek is the truth about self.

#185

SOCIAL MEDIA CAN BE USEFUL

A friend posted a video on social media as she sat in a parking lot and announced to the world she was just laid off from her job. She told her friends she needed to find employment and within a few weeks she was starting a new job. I have avoided social media for years with the exception of lurking on a few celebrities' pages. I call it lurking without committing. I didn't have to have an account to see what Rihanna wore to dinner or where Nicole Murphy went on her recent vacation. I just never really saw a point otherwise. It seemed like such a colossal waste of time and clearly I had better things to do. People would ask, "Don't you want to connect with friends from high school or from the military?" My response was, "I wasn't interested." One day a young man I mentor came to me and said, "Look, if you want to grow your empire you're going to need to use social media." After the stern talking to he gave me, I dipped my toe in the social media pool by setting up a LinkedIn page at his request or maybe it was a demand. I was thinking our roles had suddenly switched and now he was the mentor. This is what happens when you are around young people, they get so empowered they start telling you what to do. As I began to write this book a friend gave me some strong encouragement to set up additional social media accounts. It's a great way to self-promote my books, business, speaking engagements, and anything else I want the world to know. The one thing I enjoy about social media the most is the ability to reach people around the world. You can find me on Twitter and Instagram @inspired2peel.

DON'T ALLOW YOUR PAST

EXPERIENCES TO STOP YOU FROM

OPENING YOUR HEART TO LOVE

Past experiences are just that, in the past. You may be missing out on the love of your life because you are still focusing on someone from your past. The person you are still longing for is gone for a reason. When you open your heart to love, you create an energy that attracts exactly what you desire.

NEW NORMAL

Life circumstances causes people to adjust to a new normal every day. It's not an easy adjustment because it requires us to do something completely different than what we were doing before. Shifting to a new normal can be abrupt, leaving you in a state of confusion.

#188

BECOME A MENTOR

It is always a rewarding experience whenever I mentor a young person. We often complain about what they are doing wrong. We never stop to think about the fact that they may not have someone in their life to teach them what's right. We only do what we know to do until we learn to do differently. If you don't want to see young boys walking around with their pants sagging, then become a mentor and teach them how to dress accordingly. If you see a young girl who doesn't know how to present herself with confidence become her mentor. Teach her how to walk into a room and own it.

#189

REINVENT YOURSELF

In the last 3 years I started to feel like it was time to do something different. I needed a deeper meaning to my life than what I was experiencing. Doing the same thing day in and day out wasn't working; in fact I was feeling bored and uninspired. I knew there was more to my life than what I was doing. I knew there was a greater purpose I should be serving. I began to examine my skill set to see what else I could be doing. Not just to fill an empty space but something meaningful. I made a list of the things I do well without much effort or thought. I came up with the following list: effective communicator, engaging, creative, builds relationships, and professional. Much to my surprise, the list went on and on. I looked at my past jobs and careers to assist me with drafting the list. What I began to notice was a connection to everything I've ever done. The main common denominator was my love for helping people. I opened up my mental space to receive how I would continue doing so. An opportunity presented itself that put me in a position to become a Public Speaker. I utilized my gifts and skills to reinvent what I have done in the past. Reinventing yourself helps to keep you from feeling like you have run out of options.

#190

DECLUTTER YOUR LIFE

     Decluttering your life will help you to see yourself living your dreams. It's not a one- time clearing of the clutter but a lifestyle. It becomes a habit to clear out stuff that doesn't belong in order for your dreams to manifest and grow. How do you expect your garden to grow if you don't pull up the weeds. When you declutter you begin to create the life you want. Decluttering can mean anything from clearing out your physical space to decluttering your mind of the unwillingness to change. It can even mean getting rid of toxic relationships. When I say relationships it doesn't always imply a romantic one. I use to tolerate, waste time, and entertain myself with nonsense but not anymore. Too much clutter in your life causes chaos. I use to think living in chaos was normal. Most people seemingly operate well in chaos until they recognize it's not really working. I was living a life cycle of emotional chaos and confusion until one day I decided there had to be a better way. I hopped off the emotional rollercoaster and kept it moving. I knew if I didn't get out of the cycle I would be doomed to repeat it over and over again. What life cycles are you repeating because you haven't had the courage to declutter?

DON'T BE AFRAID TO SAY SOMETHING

Throughout the course of my day I see a lot of interesting things. I'm a people watcher which means I'm easily entertained by funny things people do. I saw something not long ago I wasn't too amused to see. I was driving back to my office from a lunch break when I saw a delivery truck parked on a two lane road. I waited patiently behind the truck as the driver got out to deliver the package. I watched as he flipped his wrist and the package went flying across the front yard and landed in the bushes. He was only about 5 feet away from the door steps and could have gently placed the package on the front porch. He hopped back in his brown truck and sped off like nothing had happened. I pursued him hoping the light wouldn't turn green before I had a chance to say something. I was able to get close enough to tell him to be more careful with his packages. He looked down as if he were embarrassed and said he would be more careful going forward. I know it's not always a safe thing to say something to people because everyone seems to be on edge these days. I felt comfortable enough on that particular day to say something. If you see something, say something.

#192

ASK YOURSELF A QUESTION:

WHAT IS THE TITLE OF THE

NEXT CHAPTER OF MY LIFE?

You have the power within you right now to create the life you want. But before you can do that you must be clear about what you want to see. Get a pen and piece of paper and write down what you want to see in the next chapter of your life and be sure to enclose a title.

GO DEEP

There is truth in depth. The deeper you go within the more truth you will see. I am someone who craves substance and there is so much substance in depth. Unfortunately, most people will never see it because of fear. There is very little truth on the surface which is a place where most like to dwell. My desire for substance makes people uncomfortable but I don't care because it's the substance of life that makes me happy. This is the one place where I can truly experience peace, the place where truth resides. Depth is a place where I can see the truth about all things; the truth about myself, the truth about the world, and the truth about God. I am deep, I am substance, I am peace, I am light, I am misunderstood, and I want to be around people who get it.

#194

DON'T LOOK TO OTHERS

FOR YOUR HAPPINESS

No one is responsible for your happiness but you.

DREAM BIG

When I learned to believe in myself I started to dream big. When I didn't believe in myself I didn't dream at all. A dream is a thought or idea that begins in your imagination. If a dream starts inside of you, it means you have the power within you to achieve it. All too often our dreams are being held hostage because we don't think we can achieve them. Your dreams have been held captive for too long. Free yourself from limited thinking, release your dreams and set them free. Use your imagination to live big dreams.

CONNECT THE DOTS

I was always a naturally curious person. When I was a kid I loved digging around in my pops toolbox trying to figure out how things worked. I would get toys for Christmas and by the end of the day my little fingers would be wrapped around a screwdriver taking toys apart. I went so far as to take the training wheels off my bike when my pops was teaching me how to ride. He went into the house to get something and by the time he came back, the training wheels were lying in the driveway and down the sidewalk I went on my new bike. I had a penchant for jigsaw puzzles just as I did for bikes. I loved being able to fit the tiny pieces together that seemingly didn't make sense but ultimately coming together so I could see the big picture. Life is no different. The tiny pieces of our lives in the form of our experiences and life lessons come together to reveal the bigger picture. We may not understand what these pieces mean in isolation because they don't fit. But when you connect everything you have experienced in life you will see the big picture. If you are living an awakened life, you will come to a point where everything you have ever experienced will finally make sense.

It all comes together for a greater purpose. Look back over your life and connect the dots.

#197

GET FIT

Finally, this year I proclaim to be my "Best Fit Self." The word fit has been staring at me from my vision board since 2013. I turned 50 this year so why not be the absolute best that I can be in all areas of my life. The focus of the last few years has been school, breast cancer, and my career. It's time to shift and incorporate a healthier fit lifestyle.

#198

LIVE BALANCED

I have to admit, life at times can appear to be a balancing act you just can't seem to master. One minute you're focusing on your career, and then the next minute you're focusing on school, your kids, your relationship and forget about having a social life or time for yourself. Where does the madness of it all end? How do you live a balanced life without looking like a chicken with your head cut off? In this world of multi-tasking is it possible to live a balanced life. Sometimes I wonder just how well we are doing with all this multi-tasking. Are we really accomplishing anything or are we simply going around in circles chasing our own shadow.

If we are doing well in one area of our life, you better believe something else is suffering due to lack of our attention. So what's the answer? I'm shrugging my shoulders because for a long time I didn't know. All I did know was to just keep moving. I had to figure out what would keep me balanced. You may be juggling so many things that you don't know where to start so you just keep juggling. The unfortunate thing about that approach is a life circumstance will occur, forcing you to make changes. Something usually happens to make all the things you are juggling to come crashing down. It happened to me and the only thing I could do was to sit still and wait.

I waited, and waited some more then waited some more. Finally, I was able to slowly put things back together. I didn't start the juggle game all over again because my mindset was different. I no longer had the desire to run the way I was running. I now realize I was only doing it out of necessity or so I thought. I still idle at a high pace but I don't juggle as many things as I use to. I left some things behind and focused on my purpose which helps to keep me living a balanced life. When I feel myself getting out of alignment, I quickly know how to pull it back together. It takes practice but you can totally live a balanced life. Do it now before you are forced to do so. Look for ways to move things off of your plate. Don't allow the many distractions of life to keep you from living balanced.

UNLEASH YOUR POWER

Unleash the power of the beast inside of you that's been dying to come out. We are the most powerful beings on the planet, yet we don't use it to our advantage. I have accomplished a lot in my life but I know there is more I can do. I am constantly striving to reach the next highest level of my being. I will never reach the end of my power because its potential is endless.

#200

BE AWARE OF

SELF-SABOTAGING BEHAVIORS

Self-sabotaging behaviors stand in the way of our progress, undermines our success, and can feel like the enemy within. These behaviors affect our relationships with others but more importantly it affects the relationship we have with ourselves. My two biggest self-sabotaging behaviors were comfort eating and procrastination. Some people self-medicate with drugs or alcohol and others may cause injury to themselves by cutting. In relationships, a person may create constant chaos because they are afraid of being hurt. They may break up with someone before the other person has a chance to break up with them, even if the person had no intention of breaking up. Another scenario may be an employee who constantly does things to make themselves ineligible for promotion and wonders why they are constantly overlooked. We fear rejection so before something happens to validate our fears of being rejected we sabotage the situation. Be aware of your self-sabotaging behaviors because we all have them.

#201

BE HOPEFUL

Even when you see no signs of hope, be hopeful.

I AM NOT A FINISHED PRODUCT

Just because I have reached a certain level of self-transformation, doesn't mean I am a finished product. I will continue to grow and evolve.

#203

WORDS HAVE POWER

Words have the power to uplift and words
have the power to deflate. Are you mindful of how
you use your words? Not just the words you use
with others but the words you use about yourself.
Our voice is one of the most powerful things we
possess. I now know I was gifted with a voice to
teach, heal, and change people's lives simply by
using my words. For a long time I didn't know I
had this ability. I never really felt I had a voice at
all because it was taken away from me at such an
early age. Once I became aware of my purpose, I
knew I had to reclaim my voice. I did that, and
picked up my confidence and my personal power
along the way.

#204

ASK YOURSELF A QUESTION:

WHAT IS MY QUALITY OF LIFE?

Your quality of life can be anything you want it to be. You just have to decide what you want it to be.

LIFE GETS BETTER ALL THE TIME

You have to be on constant look out for the better life you seek. There are signs along the way pointing you in that direction. You have to believe if you take a step towards your better that it will continue. You can't get discouraged when things don't look as you think they should. I have witnessed countless times when people faced with major challenges have come out triumphant on the other side. Life isn't designed to be easy, it's designed to be. If we can learn to just be with life instead of resisting, then it will get better with time.

#206

YOU CAN HAVE MORE PEACE,

MORE JOY, AND MORE HAPPINESS

Having more peace, joy, and happiness is possible. The moment you decide that's what you want and willing to do the work then it will be so. If you don't have those things now then fake it until you make it. I had to convince myself that's what I wanted until it actually happened. Now, I live in a constant state of peace, joy, and happiness.

#207

ASK YOURSELF A QUESTION:

AM I A NEGATIVE PERSON?

If you look in the mirror and recognize yourself as the negative person, you might want to figure out what you need to do to transform from that space. I looked at myself in the mirror and didn't like what I saw reflecting back at me. I was the negative person.

DO IT AFRAID

If you want to do something in life but you are afraid to do it, do it afraid. What's the worst thing that could happen if you do it and it doesn't work? What's the best thing that could happen if you try it and it does work? Worst case scenario versus best case scenario, you decide. If you never do it you will never know. To me, that is the worst case scenario.

#209

IGNITE THE FLAME INSIDE OF YOU

Doing something you love, something that drives you, something you just have to do or your world would cease to exist; this is called your passion. I feel this way about public speaking. I know I have a responsibility to raise the consciousness of humanity by using my words. God gave me that assignment long before I came to this planet and it's been burning in my soul ever since. Go within yourself to rediscover what God told you and ignite your flames of passion.

#210

DO IT EVEN WHEN YOU

DON'T FEEL LIKE IT

The first thing comes to mind is working out. Those are usually your best work outs when you don't feel like doing it. When you finish you will be glad you did it. Identify the thing you don't feel like doing and just do it.

A PATHWAY APPEARED

A few days after talking with a friend about a recent celebrity news feed, I had an epiphany. We were discussing an interview published about a sports figure who spoke about his spiritual walk. I was at a crossroads in my life and knew I had gone as far as I could go on the path I was currently walking. Something about the conversation had a profound impact because about a month later I began walking on a new unfamiliar path. It was unlike anything I had ever experienced before. A pathway to my purpose appeared.

#212

ASK YOURSELF A QUESTION:

WHAT CAN I DO TO CREATE MORE

FUN, EXCITEMENT, AND VIBRANCY?

Surely we weren't meant to live a boring life. We have to go out in the world to create the more that we want.

ASK YOURSELF A QUESTION:

WHAT MORE CAN I BE DOING?

You are never finished, there is always going to be more to do. When you accomplish a goal, there is more to do. When you fulfill a dream, there is more to do. When you transform your life, there is more to do. You will never get to a point in your life when you have nothing to do.

ASK YOURSELF A QUESTION:

WHAT IS MY PURPOSE?

Focus on your strengths because your
purpose is hidden in your gifts, talents, and skills.

DESCRIBE THE DECADES OF YOUR LIFE

I began to reflect on the decades of my life as I was about to enter a new one, I would be turning a half of a century. Wow! It sounds really old for someone like me because I have such a young spirit, and most people don't believe it when I tell them my age. Sometimes, I say it intentionally just to see the response. I'm kind of funny that way. When people look at me with disbelief, I usually say, "What woman do you know lies about being 50 years old, no one I know." So as I was rapidly approach the big 50, I did a deep review of my life by the decades. I thought about the first half of my life and it seems as though I was searching but not really knowing why or for what. I now know I was searching for meaning. My teens consisted of sitting in my room for hours watching public television, listening to motivational speakers like Les Brown and Deepak Chopra. They spoke positive words of how you can change your life. My twenties were a bit more complex. Much of the time was spent trying to sort out what I should be doing with my life and where it was headed. My thirties were adventurous and fun and not too much time for contemplating life. My forties were filled with cultivating my inner self and strengthening my relationship with God. My fifties are going to be the most amazing decade ever because I plan to use these 365 hidden treasures to build my empire. I will allow God to take my life to the next level in whatever manner He chooses.

LISTEN TO YOUR GPS

Not the GPS on your phone or in your car but your **G**od **P**ersonally **S**peaking GPS. Look to God to guide you through each day and He will.

MY BREAST TRIED TO KILL ME

ATTENTION LADIES!!!

Get your mammograms and follow up if needed. Whenever I share my story as a breast cancer survivor during a speaking engagement, inevitably someone will come up to me and say they are a survivor or knows someone who is a survivor. I spoke to a woman after a graduation who said she had a mammogram over a year ago and was advised to come back for a follow up because the doctors had some concerns. She was too afraid to hear what the doctors had to say. Just because you are afraid doesn't make the situation go away, if anything it makes it worse. She said she even received a certified letter stating she needs to come in for a follow up. I encouraged her to see her doctor and go along with whatever treatment recommendations were necessary. I knew another woman who disclosed she felt a lump in her left breast around the same time I was diagnosed but she was too afraid to find out what it was. She then told me breast cancer runs in her family, unlike me who had no history in my family. I begged her to go to the doctor to find out what was going on but to my knowledge she never did. One of the leading reasons why women die of breast cancer is because it goes untreated. If the doctors catch it at an early stage then your chances of surviving are much higher. I was diagnosed at Stage 0 and sought immediate treatment.

BE READY

If you stay ready then you don't have to spend a lot of time getting ready when your moment to shine arrives. It's like the kid standing on the sidelines waiting for the opportunity to get in the game to show what he can do. When the coach finally decides to put him in the game he better be ready. It's too late to get ready once you're in the game. When your big opportunity comes, you better not miss it because it may not come around again.

SOMETHING GOOD WILL

HAPPEN TO ME TODAY

This is my new life mantra. I wake up every day with the expectancy of something good happening. Just by the mere fact I have the expectancy, I am able to attract good things into my life. I know the word good can be somewhat relative in that we all have a different understanding of something good happening. Something good for some could be winning the lottery and for others it could be taking their first steps after being told you will never walk again. On an ordinary day I got a flat tire on the way home from work but it was still a good day. Some of you may think what's so good about getting a flat time. Well, just keep reading. It was totally my fault that I got the flat tire. I was pulling into a gas station and hit the curb. I felt that all too familiar feeling because it's happened before. I held my breath with the anticipation that my dashboard wouldn't light up telling me I had a flat tire. Just as I suspected, the light came on to alert me about the tire. I thought I was being smart and proactive by keeping a can of tire flat in the trunk of my car. I hopped out of the car and attached the can to my tire thinking it would in inflate but nothing happened. I called for roadside assistance and the tow truck was there in about 30 minutes. During my wait for him to show up, I called to see if I could have a new tire installed which was a long shot since it was rapidly approaching 6 o'clock in the evening. I spoke to a nice guy named Tim who advised the tire I needed was out of stock. He then searched for the tire in a few nearby counties and came up empty. He ordered the tire to be delivered within 24 hours.

The next day the tire arrived and things were back to normal. My baby and I were ready to hit the streets again. A few days later I received one of those annoying surveys to complete via email. I ignored it but left it my inbox with the intention to delete it at a later date. Quite unusual for me because I usually delete emails immediately that I don't need. About a week passed and I saw the survey staring me in the face so decided to complete it. Another week passed and I received a call one early morning while I was at work. I answered with hesitancy because I generally don't answer calls with no name attached to the phone number. I heard a gentleman on the other end asking if this was Loronda Giddens. He went on to ask about a recent service at one of his tire stores and to let me know I had won a $500 gift card for completing their survey. He rattled off some legal mumbo jumbo as I walked around outside in a daze. Going outside to talk is always a good idea when you don't want your co-workers in your business. I was elated after it settled in; I had never won anything like this in my life. But I felt something inside telling me this was going to become my new normal. I read something on social media a few weeks back that read "You are about to enter a season of consecutive wins." When I say the day I had the flat tire was a good day, it was because I woke up with the expectancy of something good happening to me.

MOVEMENT IS NECESSARY

When I was a probation specialist, I would always tell my kids when they came to my office each week that I wanted to see some movement from the previous week. The type of movement I was looking for was a job application completed, community service completed or any other task they were assigned to complete. I wanted them to develop the habit of setting goals and accomplishing them. Some kids talked to their teacher about doing extra credit work to improve their grades, other kids signed up for a tutor afterschool and some kids who had jobs opened a savings account. Movement is necessary if you want to get closer to having the dream life you want.

ASK YOURSELF A QUESTION:

AM I MAKING PROGRESS?

As 2015 came to a close, a friend was cleaning out her closets and came across an old wallet stuffed with papers from several years ago. She was concerned she hadn't made any progress in her life because her old wallets and purses resemble the ones she currently carries. Papers stored in a certain manner with the same type of information. I told her there was no cause for alarm. I think in general we all have a certain way of doing things. I like to think of it as being consistent. I can look back at something I wrote over 10 years ago and it would still be something I would say today. Get clear about the difference between making progress and knowing your personal style of doing things. It can be confusing and lead you to think you aren't accomplishing anything. I did reassure my friend of her many accomplishments and the personal growth I've seen since knowing her.

LIFE IS NOT MEASURED

BY MATERIAL SUCCESS

Success for me is measured by the content of my personal evolution. Material things can be gone in an instant but my evolution will continue.

#223

WHEN IT'S TIME, IT WILL BE

There is a designated time when all things are to happen in our lives. We have to be patient until the time arrives, but no one wants to hear be patient. In our microwave society we want it when we want it. Well guess what, no matter how bad we may want something we may not be ready to receive it.

#224

ONCE I AM AWARE THAT I AM

AWARE, I CAN NO LONGER BE UNAWARE

Once you have seen something it can no longer be unseen. Now that you are aware of the changes needed to transform your life you can no longer be unaware. What will you do with your new awareness?

WE LOST ANOTHER LEGEND

Prince Rogers Nelson dies at the age of 57. It's not unusual for people to die because it happens every day. It just seems as of late many of our music legends are leaving this planet, first David Bowie and now Prince. I wonder what is going in heaven that everyone wants to be there. Then it brings my thoughts to my own mortality because I'm thinking more and more I have no time to waste. I have to pursue my dreams now. Not tomorrow but right now I should be doing something to get me closer to where I want to be. No procrastination, no excuses, just focus, and do it.

#226

BE AN INSPIRATION

Being an inspiration is having the ability to awaken a particular feeling in someone. I feel I am blessed with the gift to inspire people to their highest level of greatness.

#227

ASK YOURSELF A QUESTION:

AM I LETTING MY LIFE HAPPEN?

We get up, we go to work, we come home and then we repeat the same cycle every single day. How boring! Life is truly more exciting than just repeating a series of life cycles. There are points in your life when you make things happen and there are points when you are letting things happen. Making things happen means you are doing your part. Letting things happen means after you have done your part then you allow God to do His part. Don't get in the way to try and control the outcome of what you think it should be. Let go and just let it happen.

YOU GET SIGNS OF

CONFIRMATION ALONG THE WAY

Whenever I see the signs I make sure to acknowledge its presence. Showing the Universe you recognize the signs of confirmation along the way will only ensure they will continue to be revealed. Recognizing the signs also increases your level of awareness. There isn't a single day that goes by that I'm not assured I am on the right path. Pay attention to your life to receive your signs of confirmation.

ASK YOURSELF A QUESTION:

WHAT MOTIVATES ME?

Motivation is an internal thing I into tap into with no influences from the outside. Although, I have listened to motivational speakers most of my life I have never been motivated by any of them. I have been inspired but not motivated. I often correct people when they refer to me as a motivational speaker. I see myself more of an inspiration than a motivator. Motivation is an intrinsic value that each individual has the ability to reach within to access.

#230

NURTURE YOUR CREATIVE ENERGY

Creative energy is a critical component in living your purpose. Creative energy is the place where all of your ideas flow. I have made it a practice to take a week off from work every few months to regroup. During that time I sleep, I cook great meals, lounge around doing nothing, and I do lots of writing. When I come back to work my mind is sharp and I'm well rested and less cranky. Many of the things I do on my week off are what I normally do anyway but it's good to step away to center myself. I am always mindful to stay in the flow of my creative energy.

#231

LOOK FOR THE RAINBOW

The storms of life don't last always. When the clouds lift, enjoy the rainbow that appears.

LIVE YOUR PURPOSE

There will come a point when you start walking on your path to purpose when things seem to come together. You feel differently and life begins to have some real meaning. Everything you do makes sense. You are co-creating your life with God and everything you ever dreamed of is revealing itself every single day.

BECOME TEACHABLE

Each day I set out to learn something new. I marvel at the idea of knowing something I didn't know before, especially if it's something about me. We don't know everything, even in times when we think we do. Open yourself up to allow new information to float into your mental space. Even when you want to resist the newness, let it sit for a while and see what happens. Resist the urge to resist. You know the feeling of how good something tastes the next day after the juices have had time to settle. The same thing occurs with new information. Your consciousness elevates when you learn and when your consciousness elevates self-transformation is inevitable. Get accustomed to becoming a teachable lifelong learner.

JUST BREATHE

When you don't know what else to do, stop and just breathe.

#235

KNOW YOUR WORTH

When you don't know your worth you will accept anything someone has to offer.

IT MIGHT BE YOU

If you're unhappy in every situation that you're in, you may want to take a look at the common denominator. You are the common denominator in all situations so it might be you.

#237

ASK YOURSELF A QUESTION: WHO AM I?

After much self-examination and contemplation, I know at the core of my being I am a good person. If you had to describe yourself in the 3 words what would they be? My 3 words would be; loyal, no nonsense, and confident.

MY FAVORITE PART OF THIS JOURNEY IS

The 365 lessons and beyond that I have learned.

WRITE IT DOWN

Write it down when you have a great idea. I started writing my first book on my blackberry several years ago. I had a lot of great thoughts first thing in the morning and my phone was the closest thing to me. I was looking through a notebook from 2002 when I first began writing the framework for my next book. I wrote down the table of contents and outlined what I wanted to say in each chapter. I went so far as to jot down what I wanted the book design to look like. It appears the things I wrote down are now manifesting. Not everything, just the things directly associated with my purpose. When I started writing this book in December 2015, I referred back to my notebook only to find a page titled "upcoming plans 2002 to 2005." I wrote down a plan to earn a master's degree and wanted to become an educator as well as a mental health counselor. Many years later I did earn a master's degree and worked with teens in the capacity of mental health counseling. I also became a Certified Instructor who teaches prevention education awareness. On my subconscious internal vision board my dreams were being realized but it wasn't until I became aware that it manifested in my reality. My dreams and life purpose are one.

JUST RIDE

I was on a teambuilding adventure with my agency who decided to take us zip lining. I often think of myself zip lining through the rain forest in some exotic out of country location. This was the perfect opportunity for me to practice. I thought it would be a one-time zip across the sky when I was told we were going on a canopy tour. Canopy tour, what is that? Did I fail to read the many emails in previous weeks detailing exactly what we would be doing? Apparently, I didn't read everything. I got over the initial shock that I would be going on a virtual hiking trip suspended several feet in the air. Then I was able to get into the groove of what I was about to do. Did I mention I was afraid of heights and that I had about 10 zip lines or more just waiting for me? As I stood on the ledge of the first zip line platform, the guy gave me a few instructions before I took the big plunge. All I could here was the sound of Charlie Brown's teacher's voice in my head, "Wah wah wah wah wah wah."

Finally, I snapped out of it when I heard the instructor say, "Ok you are all set to jump now." I secretly was hoping he was talking to my teammate standing at the launch pad next to mine. I looked up and he was talking to me. I felt like I was in a daze.

I was looking around at the beauty of nature and a squirrel climbing in a tree behind me. I was thinking what is a squirrel doing this high up in the trees. I know, I'm stalling and stalling and stalling. I panicked a little thinking I can't do this. But then I thought about my Director who was standing nearby and she's real competitive. I would never be able to live this down if I didn't jump. So I did, I jumped. I was exhilarated and scared as hell at the same time. It was kind of funny because I tried to stand up in my harness as if that would stop me from plummeting to the ground if it were to be my fate. After a few seconds of reckless thinking I pulled myself together to remember what the instructor told me to do. He said, "Just ride." I sat back in my harness and I did just that, I went along for the ride. After several jumps I became more comfortable and looked forward to the next zip line. It was the most fun I had in a long time. I love my team. They are the best people on the planet. We are all dedicated to making the lives of children better.

The final jump was the most divine of them all. It was a 900 foot line across Snake Creek with waterfalls in the background amidst a bevy of luscious green trees. I felt as if I were jumping into the arms of God. As I soared across the sky at high speed, I was mindful to be present to take in the absolute pure beauty of nature. I wanted the moment to last forever. All I could think to do is "just ride." On my drive home I was recapping my adventure and thinking how cool it is to just ride.

It's challenging sometimes in life to just ride. Everyone wants to be in the driver's seat, with false thinking they are in control of their lives. The day I realized I could only go so far doing things my way, I gladly got out of the driver's seat and hopped in the passenger seat to just ride. God lets me know when He wants me to do something. I now take instructions very well, before not so much. Co-creating my life with God is the perfect and only solution.

#241

CREATE SOMETHING

THAT CHANGES THE WORLD

Shifting energy elevates consciousness and raises the vibration. Raising vibrational energy causes transformation. I feel I owe the Universe something in return for the creation of my life. My something is showing people how possible it is to transform their lives. This book you are reading is an homage to my life and my legacy. I wanted to create something I could look back on several years from now and smile about all of the wonderful memories. I want people to read this book and be inspired to do more, be more, and try more things.

ASK YOURSELF A QUESTION: WHAT IS

THE ONE THING I NEED TO STOP DOING?

This may be the very thing to unlock what's been holding you back from living your dream. Once you identify the first thing you may find there are a few others to follow. The one thing I recognized I needed to stop doing was to stop procrastinating, then the next thing was to stop being fearful, then the next thing was to stop not believing in myself. When you ask the first question, whatever it is, the answer will be revealed. Keep asking questions.

LIFE IS WHAT YOU MAKE IT

Think about a time when you felt carefree even if it was just for a moment. Now think about what it will take to make that happen again. I'm not saying you can go back and change the hands of time when you didn't have kids, debt or anything of that nature. I'm talking about a mindset. What were the things you were doing and thinking that made you have a carefree approach to life?

ASK YOURSELF A QUESTION:

WHAT IS MY MANTRA?

Mine is, just be. Be in the moment of life because this is the only moment you have. You don't have the past because it's gone and you don't have the future because it's not here yet.

YOU ARE GOOD ENOUGH

I was watching television when a woman began to describe how she was awarded a public speaking scholarship but didn't pursue it because she didn't think she was good enough. I'm sure she's not the only person who thinks they aren't good enough. Thinking you aren't good enough leaves your dreams deferred, unfulfilled, and unrealized.

#246

ASK YOURSELF A QUESTION:

WHAT WOULD I DO IF I

KNEW I WOULDN'T FAIL?

This question will absolutely lead you to the road of rediscovering your passion which leads to the rediscovery of your purpose.

WATCH TV

I hear people say all the time I don't watch television as if it's beneath them. It all depends on what you're watching. I get tons of inspiration from watching television. I find myself on the OWN network quite often because Oprah is always offering up a spoon full of inspiration. It's like taking a good dose of medicine for my soul. If you can't get inspired by a Master Class or a Super Soul Sunday session then where can you go to get inspired? It's just something about the storytelling of the guests on those shows that feeds my spirit. I watch local news sparingly to stay abreast of what's going on, but I steer clear of regular viewing. I tune in to world news to know what's going on globally. I use to be able to wander off into Nerdland with a cup of French vanilla coffee and watch Melissa Harris Perry on Saturday and Sunday morning. Her show featured the best panel talk with scholars, activists, and political talking heads. But since it was taken off the air I have a hole left within me that hasn't been filled.

PUSH PAST "I NEVER THOUGHT

I COULD DO IT" AND JUST DO IT

The Nike brand made the words famous but you can apply it to your everyday life. The words aren't reserved exclusively for athletes. I know it sounds like a cliché to hear you can do anything you want if you put your mind to it, but it's true.

#249

THERE IS A SPACE BETWEEN WHERE

YOU ARE AND WHERE YOU WANT TO BE

The space is called preparation. The preparation can be the self-work of personal transformation, a formal education or simply learning how to sit still until your moment arrives.

ASK YOURSELF A QUESTION:

WHAT DO I NEED TO IMPROVE?

I don't particularly like the word weaknesses, which is why I didn't ask what are your weaknesses. I feel the word weakness disempowers. Be mindful to use words that empower yourself and others.

#251

FOCUS ON WHAT YOU DO WELL

What you don't want to do is get into the habit of discounting the great things you do no matter how small or large they may be. Learn to empower yourself by focusing on what you do well. It helps to build momentum for constant forward movement.

#252

THERE IS NO COMFORT

IN THE COMFORT ZONE

At some point your comfort zone is going to get very uncomfortable. When God wants you to grow He makes you uncomfortable.

YOU HAVE TO PRACTICE

You don't get good at something if you don't practice. If you want to learn more about how to be in the moment, practice. If you want to show more kindness to others, practice. If you want to show more compassion to others, practice. Practice kindness and compassion on yourself first then extend it to others.

ANTICIPATE

Every morning I wake I receive 2 precious gifts. The first gift is pretty obvious; it's the gift of life. The second is my beautiful red cardinal Dale. He has me so trained that I quickly open the blinds and window in anticipation of his arrival. I can hear him chirping in the distance then he gets closer and closer. Next thing I know he's outside my window within about 5 minutes. He walks around on the roof then comes closer to the window to look in at me then flies off until the next day. Sometimes he will come back a second time when he really wants his presence known. I wake up with the anticipation of something good happening. I am certain when Dale arrives each morning he will show up with my gifts from God. He brings me creativity, he brings ideas, and he brings me peace in knowing that all of my dreams are coming true.

#255

ASK YOURSELF A QUESTION:

WHAT DO I WANT?

Often times when people are asked what they want in any given situation, the usual response is, "I don't know." How can you possibly attract what you want in your life if you haven't defined it?

"When you want something all the Universe conspires to helping you to get it"

- Paulo Coelho, Author of "The Alchemist"

YOU ARE EVERYTHING

YOU ARE SUPPOSE TO BE

You were born with everything you needed to fulfill your life purpose. The better person you strive to be already resides within. Peel back the layers of your life and have it revealed.

MY FEAR LEFT AND

DIDN'T EVEN SAY GOODBYE

My fear of heights went away without me knowing it left. I was suspended hundreds of feet in the air on a zip line tour, climbing on cables and tiny pieces of wood to get to the next canopy. As I looked around to enjoy the beautiful sights and sounds of nature, my fear was nowhere to be found. My fear of heights left and didn't even say goodbye. Where does fear come from anyway? Are they just repeated irrational thoughts or does experience teach us to be fearful. Perhaps if we knew the origin of fear we could control how we respond to it. Instead of being paralyzed by fear we can successfully navigate through it. We were born to fear things; it's a natural part of who we are. Fear is helpful because it alerts us to impending danger. We have to react quickly when danger appears. The type of fear I am talking about is the fear that holds us back from pursuing our dreams.

IDENTIFY WAYS TO RELEASE STRESS

Stress will kill you if you let it. You have to find the stress reliever that works best for you, preferably something non addictive in nature. My stress relievers are yoga and meditation. It helps me to stay in my Zen happy place.

#259

DON'T CREATE A WOUND IN

SOMEONE THAT MAY NEVER HEAL

We have all heard the phrase "hurt people hurt people." Inevitably someone will be hurt by our actions. All I'm saying is not to go around hurting people intentionally. Be aware of others feelings and take them into consideration.

#260

BECOME AN ENTREPRENEUR

Not everyone has the desire to have their own business but for those of you who do, do it. I have known folks who out of necessity due to economic down turns and poor labor force started a business. I have always admired people who start up a new business in a heartbeat without hesitation. If you want to become an entrepreneur and don't know what type of business to start then think about your life purpose and start there. For instance, if your purpose is to help people then I'm sure you can start a business that will serve that purpose. Get your creative juices flowing and think outside of what you normally do. Don't limit your capabilities.

FOCUS ON WHAT'S IMPORTANT

It's hard to focus on your dreams when distractions are so loud that they drown out the deeper calling from within. You have to decide if the distractions are more important than having the life you want. I will let you determine what your distractions are but just to name a few; dead end relationships, dead end jobs, and dead end friendships. You can't revive something that's dead so why focus on it.

USE YOUR MENTAL STRENGTH

You have to push using your mental strength. You may think you don't have mental strength but we all do. We can access it by tapping into our inner resources. Your mental strength comes from the life lessons you have learned. Every time you do well and it makes you feel good about yourself, you are building mental strength. It gives you the confidence to know you can handle anything that comes on your path. One of the things I draw upon to flex my mental strength is the day I graduated from basic training in the Army. It was a challenging time when I had to use everything I had to jump that hurdle.

TAKE NOTES

I can remember as far back as high school how much I loathe taking notes. I didn't do much note taking in undergraduate or graduate school either. Now it seems like I'm always writing something down. I get inspired in the moment during general conversation and find myself making note of something being said. During conferences I take a lot of mental notes on strategies of how to elevate my own platform. If you are taking notes, what are you writing down and why?

#264

I AM MULTI-DIMENSIONAL

You have to be multi-dimensional. You have to be able to do more than one thing well. The days of doing one job until you retire are over. I can't imagine working on a job until I retire unless it's my own business. Even then I will continue to do what I love for the rest of my life.

#265

THE JOURNEY NEVER STOPS

If you think your journey ends once you accomplish your dreams then think again. The journey simply continues because you will be introduced to new levels in your dreams you never knew existed. Your dreams are multi-dimensional and what you see on the surface of your dreams is just the beginning.

KIDS ARE RESILIENT

I have worked with kids for the past 15 years who didn't grow up in the most ideal situations. It is commonplace for them to experience violence in their homes and communities. They strive and persevere despite their surrounding circumstances. These kids have dealt with things most of us will never experience in a lifetime, yet they continue to move forward. On May 20, 2016, the Georgia Preparatory Academy graduated 90 students during their spring ceremony. The Preparatory Academy is the 181st school district in Georgia housed within secure detention facilities. Students were celebrated for accomplishing such a great milestone in their life. The young men and women stood tall, walking proudly across the stage as their names were called. The valedictorian brought everyone to their feet as she addressed us with an arousing speech of hope. Kids in detention are not throwaways as most people would like to think. Kids in detention are smart, they are creative, and they are resilient.

STOP DWELLING IN LOW FREQUENCIES

      I am instinctively drawn to people who operate at a higher frequency. Elevate your consciousness by expanding your knowledge of self. Rise above negative thinking and think a new positive thought.

#268

DON'T MEASURE YOURSELF

BY SOMEONE ELSE'S SUCCESS

What God has for you is for you and you only. You don't know the struggles of the person for whom you are measuring your success. There is nothing wrong with looking at successful people and wanting to attain similar levels of success. But if you're looking at others thinking you will never be as good as this person then it becomes a problem. Stay in your lane.

#269

BE MINDFUL OF YOUR ENERGY

There are some energy vampires out there just waiting to suck you dry of your energy, so don't be so eager to give it away. Energy vampires are those people who know you have great energy and they want it. I don't mind giving of myself but don't just plug in and take what you want without giving anything in return. I believe in sharing my energy but I also believe in reciprocity.

#270

GET AQUAINTED WITH

YOUR HIGHER SELF

Your higher self is the highest expression of who you are, the best you that you can be. Through your higher self you can achieve extraordinary things. Your higher self is where your purpose resides.

#271

TEACH PEOPLE HOW TO TREAT YOU

Don't be a doormat for people to wipe their feet on. Believe me; if you let them they will do it. Sometimes you have to give people a quick lesson on how to treat you. But first you must know how you should be treated before you can communicate it to others.

ASK YOURSELF A QUESTION:

AM I OVERCOMMITTING?

I had to gradually learn that I can't do everything. I found myself doing more than I needed to be doing but not really accomplishing anything meaningful. It's okay to say no sometimes.

#273

ASK YOURSELF A QUESTION:

ARE YOU ON PAUSE, STOP, OR REWIND?

Sometimes God presses the pause button and other times He presses the stop button. In either case He does so in order to get your attention. When God pressed the stop button on my life, the only thing I could do was sit still and breathe. Some years later He pressed the fast forward button and I feel like I'm on an accelerated path of doing His will.

#274

MASTER THE RULES OF THE GAME

What game, the game of life. How often does it occur that when you learn the rules of the game they change? Don't ever get too comfortable with the rules because inevitably they will change. The game of life is change and you can master it by simply learning to embrace it.   Sometimes you can tell when change is coming and other times you get blindsided by it. If you are okay with change happening in your life then you will always be prepared when it arrives.

ASK YOURSELF A QUESTION:

AM I VISUALIZING MY BETTER?

What does your better life look like, feel like, smell like, and taste like? My better looks like gold blanketing everything I see, it feels like 100% percent imported silk, it smells like star gazer lilies, and tastes like the finest of French champagne.

There was a time when I had no vision of what my better looked like. Every time I would get a glimpse of my better, it would get covered up by a layer. You know those layers we talked about earlier in the book. It was life lesson #64 Layers Covering Your Purpose. Life circumstances would happen and I would lose sight of my better. I was at a point when I started to believe my better didn't exist. I attended a life changing women's retreat in 2013 and something in me shifted. I cried most of the day as I listened to speaker after speaker talk about their life experiences. At some point I could feel a light of hope entering my body temple and instantly knowing my better was possible. The vibrational energy in the room was so strong that I could no longer deny the transformational breakthrough happening without my participation. The only thing I did that day was to show up and be present in the moment. In the midst of my tears and depression I was present enough to recognize I wanted to be able to provide a space where women could go to become self-aware, heal, and transform. I clearly saw the vision of myself facilitating a women's retreat in the very cabin I was sitting. It was as if I was having an out of body experience. I could see myself standing before a group of women speaking on something profound to change their lives. You have to see yourself living your dream. I feverishly took notes of what I would do to make my retreat even better.

ASK YOURSELF A QUESTION: WHAT

HAVE I ACCOMPLISHED THIS YEAR?

Now, here's where the question requires you to peel back the layers and dig a little deeper. Are any of those accomplishments connected to your dreams that serve your purpose?

On May 21, 2016, a women's empowerment retreat I had dreamed about for 3 years and planned for during the first quarter of 2016 never happened. Why, because no one registered to attend. Am I disappointed? Maybe just a little bit. Will I allow it to stop me from organizing another one? No. I will just do a few things differently the next time around. Even though you work hard to accomplish something, it doesn't mean it will happen like you envision.

ASK YOURSELF A QUESTION: WHAT

IS MY TRUTH AND WHAT IS MY LIE?

What do you believe about yourself? Did you grow up believing a lie someone told you about yourself? I have heard young people say they have heard all of their life they will never amount to anything. It was told to them by teachers, their neighbors or even family members. I was watching a news story where a teacher told a young girl she was the stupidest person he ever met. He went on to tell her she was only good for having sex and making babies. I can't imagine a teacher saying something like that when I was a kid. Adults sometimes don't understand the impact they have on a young person's life. It can be a life time of devastation if that child doesn't have a strong sense of self and believes everything the adult tells them. Everyone doesn't have the ability to filter out negative things people say. If they start to hear it often enough they will begin to believe it. There is a quote that says "It's not about what people call you but what you answer to." It's also what you believe about yourself.

#278

ASK YOURSELF A QUESTION:

HOW AM I USING MY I AM LANGUAGE?

Are you saying this?

I AM STUPID

I AM UNDESERVING

I AM WORTHLESS

I AM UNLOVABLE

I AM _____ (FILL IN THE BLANK)

Or are you saying this?

I AM SMART

I AM DESERVING

I AM WORTHY

I AM LOVABLE

I AM_____ (FILL IN THE BLANK)

ASK YOURSELF A QUESTION:

WHAT IS YOUR WHY?

Asking yourself questions is a critical component to understanding your motivation. It's the reason why you do what you do. Why do you get up every morning to go to a job you don't particularly care to do. Is it because you have to pay bills or do you just want to get out of the house. Imagine if you were doing something you love and had a passion for, how much more fulfilling your life will be.

ASK YOURSELF A QUESTION:

WHAT'S STANDING IN THE WAY?

Is it you? If the answer is yes then GET OUT OF THE WAY! Get out of your way so you can experience the life you really want. You don't have to simply dream about having a better life, you can actually have it.

ASK YOURSELF A QUESTION:

WHAT AM I DOING WITH MY DASH?

When a person transitions to the afterlife, there is a memorial here on earth in the form of a headstone for those who choose to be buried. The family will often write a scripture or other kind words symbolizing who the person was. It also has the date you came into the world and the date you transitioned. But into between those two dates is a dash. The dash represents your lifetime on this planet. What are you doing with your dash? Are you doing something meaningful or are you wasting it away worrying about something that happened in the past you can't change?

#282

KNOW WHEN TO TAKE

ADVICE FROM YOUR MOTHER

If had listened to my mother I would still be working in a corporate career with no passion. Sure I would have more money in my bank account but no fire in my heart.

#283

WORK FOR IT

Don't just sit around thinking about being successful. Work for it to see your dreams come true.

#284

GO ABOVE AND BEYOND

Last year, I won the Above and Beyond award at work. I have never received an award of this magnitude before, and then again I have never pushed myself as hard as I have in the past two years. I started a new position with my agency as a Victim Advocate working at our Central Headquarters office. It was a big deal, kind of like the equivalent of working in the White House of state offices. So to win an award was a proud moment I will never forget. What made it even nicer was to receive a personal note of congratulations from my Deputy Commissioner, Sarah Draper. Her note and quote read:

"Congratulations on being chosen for the Above and Beyond Award! It is very well deserved! I truly appreciate all that you have done and all that you have taken on to better our division and victim services! You have truly become an integral part of the team and this agency!
Please read the quote on your award as I chose it specifically for the Above and Beyond award."

*"We are what we repeatedly do. **Excellence**, then, is not an act, but a habit."* - Aristotle

WEAR BRIGHT COLORS

When I was in high school I would always wear dark clothes. It was a great representation of my mood. Now, I wear bright colors and it certainly makes a difference in how I feel. I also notice the bright colors I wear affect others as well. People often compliment the colors and tells me it makes their day.

#286

IDENTIFY THE BEHAVIORS YOU

NEED TO STOP IN ORDER TO TRANSFORM

You may be thinking my life could benefit from a complete make-over. There is something standing in the way of your transformation. In order for transformation to occur you must first be aware of why you wish to transform. Once know why then you can focus on specific behaviors. I transformed my life because I was sick and tired of being sick and tired. I wanted to be happy and there were certain behaviors I had to change. Don't expect the change to happen overnight but it will happen. Just peel one layer at a time.

THERE IS A DIFFERENCE BETWEEN

SELF-ABSORBED AND SELF-AWARE

People have a tendency to think if they are self-aware they are being self-absorbed. Self-absorbed is an individual who thinks about themselves and nothing but themselves. They don't care about how their actions may impact others. A person who is self-aware is someone who knows what they are feeling, why they are feeling it, and knows how to properly manage it in their everyday life. A self-aware person also extends themselves to others in showing empathy for what they may be feeling. Self-awareness is taking the focus away from the outer you and placing attention on the inner. It is deep reflection and contemplation of your inner self. You can achieve this through meditation, journaling, and spending time alone with yourself. It's a scary idea for people to spend time alone. They may not like what they discover in their moments of solitude. Although we learn quite a bit about ourselves when interacting with others, we can learn even more valuable information when time spent alone. I'm an only child, so it's pretty easy for me to spend time alone. Having me time is a necessary part of my being. I can get a little cranky when I don't get my alone time. I enjoy my own company and don't mind going out to dinner by myself or to the movies and even concerts. I like the freedom to decide how long I want to be wherever I am going and when it's time to go. As much as I enjoy my own company, I enjoy the company of others just as much.

#288

GO AGAIN

When life knocks you down, get up and go again. There is no progress when you get knocked down and stay there. We have to be resilient and keep going no matter what. One of the Pastors of my church would often say "It's ok if you get knocked down but don't stay there."

#289

YOU CAN ONLY GO SO FAR ON THE

PATH DOING THINGS YOUR WAY

God's way or your way? Some chose to walk His path and co-create their life from birth. Others of us chose to do it our way and walk our own path. Somewhere along the way I decided that my way was no longer working. I did pretty well for the first 49 years but I knew there was something better. I knew God had a better plan for my life. Initially, I was focused on how God would do it because I couldn't see how He was going to turn things around. I am here to tell you that God works miracles. He purposely doesn't allow us to see our better until it's time. If we had any inclination of how God would do things we would find a way to mess it up. I have learned to let God be God and to take my hands off of the steering wheel. Trying to be in control is exhausting anyway so I'm glad God showed me a better way. It's a lot less stressful for me not having to figure things out all the time.

#290

DON'T WORRY ABOUT THE DETAILS

OF HOW GOD WILL DO SOMETHING

God doesn't give assignments without resources, His plan comes fully equipped. We get too caught up in how things should be done and what we think the outcome should be. When you surrender and give up control your desire to know the details will no longer exist.

AWAKE EACH MORNING

STIRRING UP YOUR GOD ENERGY

I acknowledge God's presence every morning before I open my eyes. I pray and meditate to stir up the energy that surrounds me, that runs through me and envelopes me. Everything has energy. Stir up your energy and allow it to take you places you have never been before. Your thoughts are energy, your emotions are energy, and your actions are energy. Why not use this energy to build momentum towards living your dreams.

#292

MOVE WITH A PURPOSE

TOWARDS YOUR PURPOSE

When I was in the Army during basic training, Drill Sergeant Lewis would always scream at us to move with a purpose. He wanted us to get from point A to point B quickly. He would say, "Double time soldier double time." I knew I had to run from the barracks to the chow hall to formation to wherever he wanted us to go in a swift motion. It's funny when I think about it after thirty years and those words still resonate within, it never left. It seems like now that I know my life purpose and what I'm supposed to be doing, it's like double time all over again. I'm moving toward my dreams in a rapid motion. I was walking out of the building at work when the CFO of my agency asked, "Who are you?" I told her my name and the department I worked. She then said, "You always look like you have somewhere to go." Her office overlooks the motor pool where all of the state cars are housed. Much of my time is spent on the road so I may be in and out of the motor pool 3 to 4 times a week. She probably catches a glimpse of me most of the time when she's in her office.

When you move with a purpose toward your purpose, others can see it. They may not be sure what they are witnessing but they can see the increased motion of your energy. You don't have to rush towards trying to make things happen in your life because it happens organically. There is a certain momentum that occurs when you are walking on your purpose path. It feels like your life is being accelerated. You are accomplishing things quicker than usual. Your mindset will shift to forward thinking and your consciousness begins to elevate. If you don't quite know what your purpose is, act like you have somewhere to go and it will be revealed.

ASK YOURSELF A QUESTION:

DID I RSVP TO GOD'S INVITATION?

God has been sending you an invitation to rediscover your purpose. The invitation has been the bread crumbs He drops along your path that will redirect you to your purpose. I said yes to the invitation which means God and I are co-creating the better life I know I can have. Your invitation awaits.

#294

I MOVE IN THE WORLD

BY WHAT I'M DRAWN TO

When I feel something I am moved to do something. I was drawn to brokenness. I was seeking the answer for how to fix my brokenness. I was drawn to others who were broken in hopes of being able to find a way to fix my own. It never worked because more often than not, I found myself resenting their brokenness. It turned into a situation of us exploiting each other's brokenness. I thought I could somehow fix their brokenness because they appeared too weak to do it themselves. How could I possibly think I could fix someone else's brokenness when I couldn't even fix my own? I thought my high school Psychology class gave me all the tools I needed. Little did I know that the class would become the nexus of a deeper self-assessment that took place over my lifetime.

My heart was broken, my spirit was broken and my mind was broken because I couldn't figure out how to fix all of this brokenness. I was a smart girl, I should know how to fix my own brokenness but I couldn't. So I didn't, I didn't know how to fix my brokenness because I didn't know it needed to be fixed. I thought my brokenness was "normal." It was my way of being for so long I believed that was the way it was suppose to be. I later came to the understanding that my mind was not indeed broken but waiting in stillness. It was resilient, it was contemplating, it was calculating the very moment when to snatch me from the darkness and thrust me into the light. I could only achieve this through God's grace and mercy. I use to be drawn to hurting people because I was hurting. I didn't recognize the teenage girl in me was still in need of healing. I am still drawn to hurting people but for a different reason. I want to teach people it is possible to heal your brokenness. You can transform from the hurt, you can transform from the pain, and you can transform from the brokenness.

PAIN IS A PART OF THE JOURNEY

When you came into the world, your mother endured pain for your existence. Some of us spend our entire lives trying to avoid pain. Believe it or not, it's painful trying to avoid pain. It's painful because we don't feel and when we don't feel we can't truly experience life. Pain is not easy to ignore because it shows up in our lives in so many different ways. You can experience physical pain, emotional pain, and mental pain. Like many of you, I have experienced all three and sometimes at the same time. It's interesting when you are feeling emotional and mental pain how your body starts to feel physical pain. When there are no obvious signs of why you should be in physical pain you still feel it. There is no separation of the body temple. Your mind, body, and spirit are one. The great thing about my pain was that it was temporary and eventually I did move beyond it.

One of my major breakthroughs for healing came about as I counseled a group of teen girls for a few years beginning in 2004. We had a retired art teacher who would visit with them every Wednesday. She would bring art supplies and give the girls no instructions on what they should paint. The girls would create amazing pieces that covered the walls of the entire room. As you look around you would see nothing but their insides on the walls. Everything they were feeling internally was displayed for all to see. They were raw, they were bold, they were honest, and they were vulnerable. I was gifted with the girl's artwork before the center closed due to budgetary constraints. A 16 year old girl created the below art of pain in broken pieces.

#296

ASK YOURSELF A QUESTION:

WHAT DO I DO IN A TIME OF PAIN?

Pain changes the very existence of who you are and you we will never be the same. Pain can be loss of a loved one, disappointment, or heartache. I find myself digging deep past my pain to come out of it even stronger. In my history of working with young people, I have seen the physical scars of them cutting on the arms in an attempt to relieve pain. A young girl I use to call "squirt" told me the reason why she cuts herself is because the pain is released as the blood runs out of her arm. I would see them as young as 12 years old with an arm full of scars. I saw it mainly in girls then I started to see the boys doing it as well. One young man had scars from his shoulders all the way down his arm to his wrists. These kids are cutting in places likes their stomach and inner thighs, making it more difficult to detect. The up side to this very sad story is they had therapists to work extensively with them to teach appropriate coping skills. How are you coping with your pain?

#297

NO NEED TO LABOR FOR

WHAT COMES NATURALLY

A professor I know asked God what she should be doing with her life. She had no intention to teach, she had no intention to even pursue her Doctorate. But one day a colleague called and asked if she would be interested in teaching a class. She happily obliged and that's how it happened. She didn't have to interview for the job and started teaching right away. She had no history of teaching, no experience with writing a syllabus much less knowing what she would do the first day of class. She trusted God because He obviously led her down this path for a reason. She finds no greater joy than to be able to make a difference in the lives of her students. Naturally, she had the ability within to teach.

#298

DON'T TALK YOURSELF

OUT OF YOUR GOOD

Just because you may have experienced bad breaks in life, is no reason to believe your life can't be good. We've all had bad breaks and will continue to have them; it's a natural part of life. I overheard two women talking and one was saying how she wished she had more time to do absolutely nothing. The other one chimed in and said, "That will only happen when I'm in heaven." I thought to myself how miserable I would be if I have to wait until I got to heaven to experience my good. It is possible to have heaven right here on earth.

#299

ASK YOURSELF A QUESTION:

AM I DOING SOMETHING TODAY

THAT WILL GET ME CLOSER TO

WHERE I WANT TO BE TOMORROW?

If the answer is no then you have some work to do. A dream is only a dream if it remains in your consciousness. A real dream is on display for the world to see, to feel, and touch. Allow your dream to be free and give the world the benefit of your gifts.

#300

FOLLOW YOUR INTUITION

I am a deep thinker who used to rely heavily on my thoughts. There were too many external factors influencing my thoughts so I had to shift to my internal sources to follow my intuition. My thoughts are fluid but my intuition is constant. Your intuition is there for a reason. Try using it every now and then to see how it will add value to your life.

FOLLOW YOUR DREAMS

Do something every single day that will get you closer to your dream. If you can follow the dreams of someone on social media then you can certainly follow your own dreams. Following your dreams means you are doing things you love, things that bring you joy, things you would be willing to do for free. This is how I feel about using my voice to inspire others to step into their greatness. When I'm following my dreams I find myself in an endless flow of creativity. Ideas literally tumble out of me with such ease. I get lost in a world outside of myself. I'm in my zone when I have the opportunity to create far beyond the place of my imagination. I am in a constant state of excitement about my dreams because I can see the manifestation of them coming to life.

DON'T LISTEN TO PEOPLE WHO

DON'T SUPPORT YOUR DREAMS

Do you realize it doesn't matter what other people think when it comes to your dreams. I'm amazed at how much value we place on other people's opinion of us. Sadly, I was watching a news special on the influence social media had on a group of 13 year olds. These young people were doing anything they could on social media to get as many likes from friends and even people they didn't know. I have come to realize adults are no different. I get it, we're human and ultimately we just want to know we are loved and accepted by others. But what happens if we don't get the love and acceptance we are seeking, then what? Do we cease to exist? I have seen many people who didn't have any family or friends to support them but they continued to follow their dreams anyway. You want the people closest to you to support your dreams but don't be surprised when they don't. There is hope because you will find people who will support your dreams and even be your biggest cheerleader. But until that time comes, be your own cheerleader.

#303

ALLOW YOUR IMAGINATION TO TAKE

YOU PLACES YOUR REALITY WON'T

What I'm about to say is very corny but true. If you can conceive it you can achieve it.

#304

ASK YOURSELF A QUESTION: AM I

ALLOWING FEAR TO DICTATE MY LIFE?

Fear is one of the things holding many people back from living their dreams. Before something bad happens we will spend good energy in anticipation of it happening. We spend entirely too much time worrying about things that may never happen. Just think if you spent that energy on pursuing your dreams how much you could accomplish. The same way we anticipate something bad happening, we can anticipate something good happening. All it takes is a shift in how you think.

#305

WE ALL HAVE FLAWS

I am flawed but I am centered in who I am.

#306

LIFE IS STILL HAPPENING

Depression, death of a loved one, financial struggles, mid-life stagnation, the end of a relationship or working in a job in which you have no passion. It's difficult to think positive thoughts when your mind is so consumed with more pressing issues. Pursuing goals can be challenging while life is still happening. You can overcome your struggles because they will always be there in some form or another. Fight for your dreams because it's worth it.

IF YOU DON'T DO IT, IT WON'T GET DONE

We were all born with a purpose. We were given special gifts designed specifically to help us to fulfill this purpose. If you never rediscover what they are then your purpose will never be fulfilled. Your purpose is unique unto you and there is no one else in the world that can fulfill your purpose but you. If you don't do it, it won't get done.

#308

SOCIAL MEDIA ISN'T SO BAD AFTER ALL

Despite the negative elements of social media there are some positive things I see floating around. I handle social media much like I do my own life by steering clear of the drama. I'm enjoying social media for now because I get to deliver gold nuggets to the world every day.

#309

WHAT ABOUT YOUR FEELINGS

Your feelings are just as important as the
next person. We're taught to put others first and if
we don't we are being selfish. Much to the
contrary, it's ok to put yourself first without the
guilt. As long as you don't walk around with the all
about me attitude then self-consideration is fine.

#310

TIME FOR YOURSELF

I constantly hear people talk about what they don't have time to do. Of course you have time for whatever is important. If you want more time for yourself then practice it. Instead of focusing on having an entire day to yourself, focus on having 5 minutes. Then maybe work your way up to 10 minutes then an hour and eventually you will get the entire day. If it means setting boundaries with others then do so. But if you continue to say I want more time for myself and do nothing then you will never get it.

#311

TRAVEL

Get a passport and travel. Here are a few things I have seen and done:

Caribana festival and Niagara Falls in Canada

Eifel tower in Paris

London Bridge

Atomium in Belgium

An outdoor café in Austria

Fields of tulips and windmills in Holland

Snow-capped mountains of Switzerland

Canals of Venice Italy

Smokey mountains in Tennessee

Hollywood sign and Walk of Stars in California

Golden Gate Bridge in San Francisco

Luscious sprawling vineyards in Napa Valley

South fork ranch in Dallas

Beautiful people in South Beach Miami

Princess Grace's memorial site, Monte Carlo casinos and nude beaches in the South of France

Dancing until dawn in the Italian night club Marmallata

Skiing the European Alps

Dunn's River Falls in Ocho Rios Jamaica

Catamaran sails in Martha's Vineyard

Three country cruise to England, Belgium, and Holland for my 21st birthday

#312

ELEVATE YOUR PASSION

You elevate your passion when you choose life. It's time to stop dwelling in sadness, hurt, and sorrow. Make your passion the focal point of your life and let it guide you to greatness.

#313

SIGNS ARE EVERYWHERE

If you miss the signs of life then it's your own fault. Plug in, engage and look around for the signs of life. This book in itself is a sign; something about it drew you to make the purchase. I predict Oprah Winfrey is going to love this book. It is my intention for the world to be transformed after reading it. My intention is for my readers to be inspired to think a new thought, reinvent themselves, experience restoration, rediscover their passion, and to live on purpose.

LOVE AND MONEY

Money doesn't make you happy but it does create opportunities. Money allows you to be more of who you are. If you are kind then you will be more kind, if you're selfish then you will be more selfish. I was listening to the radio and they asked people to call in to answer the question of the morning. Would you leave your relationship if you won $1.5 billion in the lottery? They only wanted callers who would leave their relationship and why. The phone lines lit up with a stream of people giving reason after reason why they would leave their relationship. Why should an abundance of money be the reason for you to leave? Why not just have the courage to leave without the money being the deciding factor. If the relationship isn't working then doesn't it make sense for both parties to move on? There was a woman who won an obscene amount of money in the lottery who kept bailing her boyfriend out of jail. She spent several thousand dollars every few weeks bailing him out. I wonder about the pathology of this guy because even with an abundance of money at his disposal he continues to commit crimes.

#315

ROAD BLOCKS, DETOURS, AND DELAYS

Don't get stuck at the road block of life. Sure setbacks will come but it's up to you what you will do with them. Will you sit wishing the roadblock will move or find a way to navigate around it? Road blocks, detours, and delays are often times designed for us to take a moment and pause for contemplation. We are so busy moving forward and running to the next thing that we miss the precious moments of contemplation.

140 CHARACTERS IS NOT WHO I AM

We read 140 characters on social media and think we know someone. We have lost the art of engagement. We don't take time to get to know one another. We assume we know a person based on what they say online. I was listening to an interview with the late Davie Bowie who said Americans are obsessed with sound bites. You hear 3 or 4 things about a person and you think you know them. What happened to the days when you could go to your next door neighbor to borrow a cup of sugar? I think those days are far behind us because we don't even engage with people in our immediate surroundings. I could be wrong but that's just something I've noticed.

DON'T EXPECT PEOPLE TO LIVE

UP TO THE EXPECTATION OF

WHO YOU WANT THEM TO BE

If you're waiting for that to happen then you will be disappointed every single time. People are going to be who they are regardless of how you feel about it. We can't waste time wishing for someone else to change, maybe the person that needs to change is you. We have to learn to respect people where they are and allow them to be who they are going to be. If it's not something you can deal with then you need to move on. Sometimes it's not that easy to move on because that person you are hoping will change is a family member. You can't exactly just trade them in for an upgraded model. You can't choose your family but you can certainly make wise choices when it comes to others you allow in your life. You DO have a choice in the matter.

ARE YOU THERE GOD, IT'S ME LORONDA

One of my favorite books as a teen was
"Are you there God, it's me Margaret?"
Sometimes we wonder if God hears us or not.
Especially after praying endless prayers with no
results. The real question is are we listening when
He does speak? Are we listening for the answers
the way we want to hear it or are we listening to
hear God's will for our life. We get so focused on
the way we want to hear it, that we miss the many
messages being sent. We want God to answer our
prayers but we want Him to answer them the way
we want them answered. Learn how God speaks to
you so you don't miss the answer to your prayers.

#319

BEST SOLUTIONS, BEST PRACTICES

THAT ARE EVIDENCE BASED

You say you don't always know the best solutions to your greatest challenges. I'm here to tell you, I am God's evidence that He is the best practice and best solution.

DON'T IGNORE YOUR LIFE WHEN IT'S

TELLING YOU TO CHANGE DIRECTIONS

If you are paying attention to your internal GPS (God Personally Speaking) you will always know where to go. Your life will call you in a different direction.

#321

EVERYTHING YOU HAVE EVER

DONE YOU HAVE NEVER DONE BEFORE

So why are you so afraid to follow your dreams? Everything that you know you had to learn how to do. The first time I spoke in front of a group was in a public speaking class in college in the late eighties. I did a presentation where I demonstrated how to make a European inspired winter cocktail called Gluehwein. The more I spoke over the years the better I became. I never knew taking that class would eventually lead me on the path of becoming a Public Speaker.

FOR NOW

Don't chase the job that pays more money when there is no passion behind what you're doing. It may be fine for now but long term you will yearn for something more.

#323

IN THE MIRROR

The late Michael Joseph Jackson had it right when he said, "Take a look at yourself and make that change." What do you see when you look in the mirror? Are you afraid to look too close because you may see something you don't like? I was afraid to look too close at myself because I knew there would be things I didn't like. People are afraid to see themselves. They are afraid of self-examination. What you're looking at isn't always pretty but is necessary for self-transformation.

#324

THE 90 DAY RULE IS REAL

ATTENTION Singles!!!

Use the 90 day rule. Take your time getting to know someone before making a major life changing decision. You can know someone for years and never really know them. But at least take the initial days to learn as much as possible. Not in a neurotic way to where you want to know everything about the person since birth in 30 minutes or less. Allow yourself to get to know someone naturally with no expectations. It takes at least 90 days to even know if you like the person enough to continue getting to know them. Sometimes it doesn't take that long if the obvious signs are present. Hint, hint: red flags!

#325

WAS WAS WAS AND IS IS IS

The past is the past and this moment is all you have.

#326

NURTURE YOUR

RELATIONSHIP WITH GOD

God is more than just a receiver of prayers. We often think God punishes us for the bad things we do, I have thought it myself. He will teach a lesson but He doesn't punish and He doesn't say I told you so.

YOU'RE NOT ALWAYS

GOING TO KNOW WHY

Some questions will remain unanswered and you have to learn to be ok with it.

WOE IS ME, WHO IS WOE?

Is woe the name on your birth certificate? If not then stop claiming it as though it were.

ASK YOURSELF A QUESTION:

HOW AM I USING MY ENERGY?

Focus your energy on getting closer to your dreams. Often times we find ourselves wasting time on situations that don't even deserve our attention let alone our energy. As you get closer to fulfilling your life purpose, your light will begin to shine brighter and brighter. People will be attracted to your light. Be mindful of the energy vampires who want to deplete you of all that good energy.

YOU HAVE TO BE WHAT

YOU WISH TO ATTRACT

You can't expect to attract something into your life if you aren't a representation of it. If you aren't attracting what you want then it may be time to do something different. We generally attract what we are emitting into the Universe. Whatever awareness and healing is needed for your transformation, you will attract life lessons to aid in the process.

#331

I AM TOO CREATIVE FOR A 9 TO 5

I saw a post on social media that read "I am too creative for a 9 to 5. It instantly stuck me because that's exactly how I have been feeling lately. I have the luxury to be creative in my 9 to 5 but there are limitations, especially as a government employee. I am fortunate to have a Director who lets me loose to do my thing. I have learned how to be creative within the confines of my limitations. I find myself having to schedule my creativity of writing and other projects around my 9 to 5. Don't get me wrong, I enjoy what I do in my 9 to 5 because I have a passion for making the lives of kids better. However, I'm itching to do it on a larger platform as an entrepreneur. I know my time is coming and my dream is right around the corner. I have to be patient a little while longer but I know its on its way. I visualize it every single day.

I noticed when I have to schedule my creativity, I may not be feeling creative in that moment. The scheduled creative moment turns into a nap or watching something mindless on television. I usually get my "float ins" when I first wake up. Which is great but then I have to stop writing or planning and get ready for work. Sometimes I have to pull over on the side of the road to capture a float in. You're probably wondering what is a float in. A float in is a really great idea that just floats into my head. I love it when it happens because it seemingly comes out of nowhere. I keep my mind free of clutter to increase the frequency of the float ins.

LIFE ISN'T ALWAYS

GOING TO BE CONVENIENT

If the only time you follow your dreams is when it's convenient then I guess you will never do it. All too often we complain about our current situation but are unwilling to do anything to change it. A co-worker was complaining about a work situation and how sick and tired he was of dealing with the same issues. I told him it appeared to me it was time for him to pursue another avenue. I asked him what he was putting off doing that he loved to do. He thought about it for a minute and couldn't think of anything. I waited and asked again but in a different way. I said, "What do you enjoy doing that you do naturally and can make money?" He smiled and said, "I enjoy working out." It was obvious to me but it took him a minute to plug in to where I was going with my line of questioning. Then we started to talk about how long it would take him to become a certified personal trainer and up pops the roadblock. He told me it would take about three months to get his certification then went into all the reasons why he can't do it right now. He talked about how the campus wasn't a convenient location to his home or second job. He had two options; he could either take three months out of his life to move towards something he loves. Or he could use the same three months to complain and not move at all. The guy is a walking billboard.

People are always asking him about his workout regime and how to go about a healthier lifestyle. Don't miss an opportunity to pursue your dreams because the road to it isn't convenient.

#333

THE BEST IS YET TO COME

As good as I feel right now, I know the best is yet to come.

WE CAN DRESS OURSELVES UP

REALLY WELL BUT EVENTUALLY

THE REAL YOU WILL EMERGE

The honeymoon period is over. The representative you show to the world can't hold out any longer and the real you starts to tumble out. Layer by layer you start to change colors like a chameleon. The person people thought you were no longer exists.

DON'T ALLOW THE NEGATIVE ENERGY

OF OTHERS FUEL YOUR DISCONTENT

If you are already feeling dissatisfaction with your life circumstances then you certainly don't need anyone else fanning the flames. Other people's negative energy can make your situation worse. I witnessed it first-hand as I was walking towards a friend who was engaged in a conversation with someone. When the person left, I noticed my friend wasn't her usual self. The look in her eyes was different than I had ever seen before. There was even a visible difference in her posture. I could tell she wasn't having the greatest of days so I advised her to just be still for a moment and breathe. I told her whatever issue she was experiencing was temporary. I also advised her to be mindful of the people in whom she shares her discontent.

TALK IN YOUR RELATIONSHIPS

Don't expect a person to read your mine. Communicate, communicate, and communicate some more. You don't have to, but if you plan stay in a relationship it would probably be a good idea. I would recommend reading Gary Chapman's book, *"The 5 Love Languages"* to discover what language you speak. You may find it difficult to communicate your love language because you may not know what it is. Love can be a tricky thing. Whenever I talk to my young people about dating relationships, I always ask them who was the first person they ever loved. The usual response is a mother or father. Think for a moment if you have a dysfunctional relationship with a parent growing up. It sets the tone for every relationship going forward. Many of my young people don't have the greatest of family support so it's challenging for them to know what love and support looks like. If every person in their life has abused or neglected them it's difficult for them to trust. Take a look underneath your own layers of distrust to figure out your love language.

#337

ROME WASN'T BUILT IN A DAY

I have been transforming since birth into the person I'm going to be.

#338

HAPPY IS A CHOICE

For many years of my life I didn't choose happy. You determine if you live a happy life. Put aside the things you have no control over and choose happy.

WRITING A BOOK IS A PROCESS

If you have aspirations of becoming an author, be patient with yourself and allow the book to unfold organically. It takes time to write a good book worthy of readership. I have seen advertisements for workshops who claim to able to teach you how to write a book in thirty days. I guarantee you if I wrote a book in thirty days it would end up as the lining on the bottom of a bird cage. You may be able to teach the process of writing a book in 30 days but actually writing the book in thirty days is a stretch. Unless the only thing you do for thirty days is write. Unfortunately, most people don't have the luxury of unplugging from their life to dedicate time exclusively to write a book. I started writing this book in December 2015 with the intention to have it published two months later on my 50th birthday. Well, two months came and went and I was still writing. My friends kept asking, "Are you finished yet?" They started to sound like little kids on a car ride, "Are we there yet?" I kept saying two more weeks; I will be finished in two more weeks. So now here we are, six months later and I am ready to release this baby to the world.

On my vision board I have the words, Worldwide: Be a part of the global experience. I am excited to know my book will be on sale through Amazon Kindle in the United Kingdom, Canada, Germany, India, France, Italy, Spain, Japan, Brazil, Mexico, and Australia. The really cool thing is I have been to at least five of these countries. Dreams do come true. You have to visualize what you want and go for it. If you want to write a book then do whatever it takes to make it happen. I went to work every day and still found the time to write. I would stay up late and wake up early. I put myself in the mindset of when I was in graduate school and had to write those long research papers. You always have to be ready to write. Inspiration will strike at any moment and you have to be ready to capture it. Some days you may not feel any inspiration at all but if you put yourself in the space of your creative energy the ideas will flow. The words will fill the page. When I wake up in the morning and finish meditating I hear words. When I'm in the shower I hear words. The words for this book literally tumbled out of me quickly but it took time to compose them the way I wanted. I use the memo section in my cell phone to capture my thoughts because it was quicker than pulling out the laptop. A recorder is also a good source to use, preferable one that translates into written words. Some people keep a notepad by their bed, but for me it was easier to use my phone because I emailed everything to myself then copy and paste it into the manuscript. You have to figure out what style works best and use it. Finish what you started authors, dust off those old manuscripts and get to

work. If your book is simply an idea, get started
writing today. You can do it.

SET THE INTENTION

Forget about your to do list and create an intention list. Setting your intention means you are committed to doing what you say you're going to do. It's more than just writing down a list of things you want to accomplish. Setting your intention means you are taking aim at something. Every fiber of your being will activate to make it so. When you set the intention and commit to what you want, the Universe will rise up to give you your heart's desire.

#341

FEEL LIFE

When I hear people say they aren't
passionate about anything it makes me sad. I can't
imagine what my life would be like if I didn't have
something to be passionate about. Long before I
knew I was passionate about helping people I had a
passion for something. When I was kid I loved
riding my bike, skating, and flying kites. I had an
even greater love for music and of course, Michael
Jackson. Those things gave me such joy and I still
have a great passion for them today. When you're
passionate about something it makes you feel. I
think as a society we are way too comfortable with
not wanting to feel for fear of getting hurt. I would
rather feel and get hurt than have no passion in my
life. I believe my passion for life is directly tied my
happiness. I wake up happy every day because I am
feeling life.

#342

ASK YOURSELF A QUESTION: WHAT

WOULD MY AUTOBIOGRAPHY SAY?

There is the story we tell the world and then there is the real story. I call the real story the back story because we keep it in the background away from prying eyes. I asked a friend who is also writing a book if she is ready to share her story. Some aspects of the story she is willing to share but other parts she's not sure. I advised her not to spend too much time thinking about it because whatever needs to be shared will come out organically during the writing process. The importance in sharing our stories is to help others to see they are not alone in their struggles. Our stories can be used as a source to inspire others to do great things. The stories I'm sharing in this book are the prequel to the back story I will share in my next book. You will get a chance to see me dig a bit deeper into my layers to understand how I was able transform to where I am today. It's not always easy sharing your life so openly because you subject yourself to criticism, judgment, and rejection. In my younger years I was intensely private and people would always say I was so mysterious. It was kind of cool being the intriguing mysterious girl people didn't know much about, especially when I first moved to Atlanta. I shared very little of myself not to be mysterious but because I didn't want people to see what an emotional mess I was. It wasn't until I figured out my own mess that I felt comfortable enough just being me. I began to understand what it meant to be authentic and I wanted nothing more than to find it within me.

#343

HEAL WHAT LIES WITHIN

Don't be afraid to see what's going on inside of you. By doing so you may be able to answer the life question, "Why do I do the things I do?" This was the question I asked myself and it opened the door to my transformation. If you don't do the self-work then the dis-ease will spill over into every area of your life causing impairment in your daily functioning. You have to go within and heal those old wounds because they are the root cause of most of our problems.

#344

THERE IS A BIGGER PICTURE

    You get pieces of the puzzle along your journey. Don't get discouraged when you can't see the bigger picture. As a kid I loved putting together jigsaw puzzles. I always went in with the same strategy. I put all the border pieces in one section then all of the matching color pieces in another. I quickly put together the pieces I knew fit and sat patiently to figure out the remaining pieces. Sometimes it took days or weeks but I kept going.

PEELING BACK THE LAYERS IS MIND

ALTERING AND LIFE CHANGING

Peeling back the layers is necessary to
liberate you from fear, shame, and guilt or whatever
layers you are carrying. Layers start to feel
comfortable even when they are uncomfortable.
We get so used to being uncomfortable that we
don't notice when we should be doing something
different with our lives. There is no particular way
to begin to peeling layers, the most important part
of peeling layers is to start. I began to peel layers
long before I knew that's what I was doing. I was
searching for answers to questions I didn't know
existed. I began to connect the dots by noticing the
seemingly coincidental things happening. I
experienced a spiritual awakening leading me to
something greater. I peeled even more layers when
I started writing. It was very therapeutic in nature.
You have to peel and heal in order to reveal the
hidden treasures of your life.

LET GO SO YOU CAN BE FREE TO FLY

Release and let go of the things that no longer serve your greatest good and highest joy. Think for a minute about the massive BP oil spill in the Gulf of Mexico in 2010. Human lives were forever changed, businesses were ruined, and the wildlife suffered. Birds had to be rescued and bathed because they couldn't fly with oil on their wings. What oil spill did you land in keeping you from being free to fly? There is strength in letting go.

ASK YOURSELF A QUESTION: WHAT

LAYERS DO I NEED TO PEEL?

Layers I had to peel were procrastination, fear, lack of self-confidence, and self-doubt.

#348

DON'T FORGET TO SAY THANK YOU

Thank you God for everything.

Thank you mom and dad for building a solid foundation for me to stand.

Thank you Bishop Dr. Barbara L. King for your spiritual guidance.

Thank you Arkeysha McCullough for your encouragement and support.

Thank you Latera M. Davis for bringing to my awareness the existence of another pathway.

#349

ONCE IN A LIFETIME

Once in a lifetime you will get the opportunity to have your moment. Don't miss it!

"Follow your bliss, find where it is and don't be afraid to follow it." - Joseph Campbell

#350

I FEEL POWERFUL

KNOWING I OWN MY NOW

There were times in my life when I felt powerless. Today, I feel powerful knowing I own my now.

LOOK FOR THE MESSENGER

When you are living an awakened life, you receive messages in many different ways. I wake up every day with expectancy of receiving a message to give me insight about my life. People always ask how do you know if God is speaking or if it's your own thinking. Once you develop a relationship with Him you will know. It's not something I can explain, it's just a feeling. Another fascinating way in which I receive messages is through Joel Osteen. Over the past 3 years it seems like Joel has been spot on and has spoken directly to me at certain points in my life. These are messages I received from Joel this year:

"God is getting ready to show out in your life."

"God is going to make your head swim."

"God is going to accelerate your life."

"God is going to make you famous and give you notoriety and wealth so you can make a difference in the world."

"God has a set time to show you favor. He will give you the platform and people will notice you."

RAISE YOUR EXPECTATIONS

Raise your expectations of yourself and others. Don't accept mediocrity, you have far too much greatness residing within. Raise your expectations of others in the way they treat you. People will only do what you allow them to do. Raise your expectations of yourself as it relates to the type of people with whom you spend your time. Do these people uplift and support you or do they deplete your energy. If the latter is true then you may want to transition from those people and surround yourself with people who get it. You want to be around people who understand your vision and are willing to help out if necessary and vice versa. Mutuality and reciprocity are two words I have on my vision board. These are expectations I had to put in front of my face as a reminder for anyone who is a part of my inner circle.

#353

ACCEPT YOURSELF

If you don't accept yourself, how do you expect anyone else to?

CO-CREATE YOUR LIFE WITH GOD

I was baptized as a kid on the same day as my father at First Baptist Church Piney Grove by Reverend Cornelius Vanderbuilt Ford. I didn't know God then. I thought God was up in heaven sitting on a thrown that you can't feel or touch but you know He's there. I have come to know that the spirit of God resides in me and I can access Him whenever I want or need to. He has his hand on my life. I didn't know that when I was being dunked under the water as the congregation watched a frightened little girl. On the outside people thought I was a tough kid because I always put up such a brave front, but a lot of the times I was afraid. God has long calmed my fears of many things. When I moved to Atlanta in 1998, I met a friend a year later who took me to the church that sat on the hill. At the time it was called Hillside Chapel and Truth Center led by Founder Dr. Barbara L. King. Now it's called Hillside International Truth Center. Dr. Barbara as we lovingly call her is known throughout the world so it only makes sense to change the name.

The life I thought I knew would no longer be the same after attending Hillside. I learned about myself and how I could have a relationship with God. Dr. Barbara went on to teach that God was inside of me and I can co-create my life with Him. Well it took me another 15 years to actually start co-creating my life with God. Dr. Barbara was laying a spiritual foundation for me to stand on firmly as I grew my relationship with God and self. In those 15 years I heard spiritual teachers such as Dr. Wayne Dyer, Iyanla Vanzant, Deepak Chopra, and others talking about co-creating your life with God. They gave detailed accounts of how it happened for them and how it changes your entire life.

It wasn't until I was diagnosed with breast cancer that I started to pay attention to my life in a real way. I knew once I was victorious over the dis-ease in my body that God had something greater for me to do so I began to search. The more I searched the more of the hidden treasures He would reveal. It was extraordinary the things He was showing me. I was overwhelmed and overjoyed at the same time. My love for Him deepened and our relationship strengthened and I knew I was on the pathway to my purpose. Once I surrendered to His will and not my will He started to show me things I had never seen before. Co-creating your life with God is probably a foreign concept for most, just as it was for me. It's not something you can intellectualize or philosophize; it's a feeling thing and you will know when it happens.

#355

THERE IS NO ONE IN THE

WORLD QUITE LIKE YOU

I have always been a bit different than most
and I use to think there was something wrong with
being different. But what I found out was that I was
perfect in the eyes of God. I have learned to
embrace my uniqueness because it sets me a part
from blending into the crowd. As an only child I
marched to the beat of my own tune and never
followed what everyone else was doing. I'm an
intensely deep thinker and I'm passionate about
what life has to offer. I like things to be a certain
way and use to think of myself as being too rigid.
Now I simply describe myself as a woman who
knows what she wants. My friends try to throw the
Diva label at me but I gracefully decline, that never
has been or ever will be me. We all have unique
qualities that define us and there is no one in the
world that can do what you do the way you do it.
Michael Jackson was a musical genius. No matter
how hard others may try to imitate his dance moves,
there will never be another quite like the great MJ.

#356

ASK YOURSELF A QUESTION:

HOW DO I MAKE DECISIONS?

Do you make decisions based on emotions or impulsively? Do you make decisions spontaneously or haphazardly? Do you analyze it from every possible angle until there is nothing left to analyze? I'm raising my hand because I use to be that girl. I looked at every possibility and ran it through my mind a million times before I came up with what I thought was a suitable answer, how exhausting. I have since been freed from the agony of making decisions in that manner. Now, I simply look for the signs in my life as to what I should do next. Most decisions are easy for me; if it's not associated with my life purpose then it's not for me. Other decisions may require me to look a bit deeper at my life. I look at what my thoughts and language has been leading up to the point of having to make the decision. The things you think about and talk about will multiple; your energy will draw certain situations into your life. If for the last six months my thoughts and words have been about writing a book then it's a pretty simple decision if I should do it or not. But just because you think and talk about something doesn't always mean it will happen. It may not be the right time or it may not be a part of your purpose.

If you pay attention to your life, you have the answers to many of the questions even before they arrive. The decision is already made before you have to make it. Decisions you make will either get you closer to your purpose or farther away from your purpose. I believe my entire life has been designed for me to figure out what I'm supposed to be doing while I'm here. The beauty is that I have all of these hidden treasures in the form of life lessons pointing me in the right direction. I feel like I have walked two paths in my life but they were always connected, just occurring at different times. The first path was the path I chose and the second path is the path I'm walking on now, my purpose path. Every decision I made on my previous path eventually led me to my current one. I'm not saying my first chosen path was the wrong one because it was essential for my evolution. I never knew another path existed until it was revealed. Once it was revealed, I have seen the guideposts showing me where to go ever since. Finding out what your particular purpose is not a thinking thing, it's a feeling thing. It's just something you know if you allow yourself to open up to receive.

I WAS USE TO FAILURE

Most of us are afraid of failing and it renders us into a state on inactivity. If we do nothing then we don't have to worry about failure. If we do something and actually succeed then the expectation level raises and we have to do more to maintain and exceed the accomplishment. I believe we have a built in expectation of failure. We feel we will fail more than we feel we will succeed. I see failure as an auto correct, as a means of making adjustments along the way when needed. If I try something and it doesn't work then I will try something else. Hopefully you will learn what not to do the next time around. Eventually, if you keep trying and don't give up you will succeed.

#358

TEACH YOUR CHILDREN

ABOUT CULTURAL DIVERSITY

I was the only black female in my high school graduating class of 405 students. I learned about cultural diversity long before it ever became a buzz word. I always find it interesting when I'm talking to a group of teens about music and inevitably someone will describe music as being black music or white music. I stop and scratch my head and wonder what does this mean exactly. I asked, "What is white music and black music?" The person who said it usually gives a long drawn out explanation that didn't make sense to me but made perfectly good sense to them. I can't blame their lack of knowledge on their adolescent status because I have heard adults describe music as being black or white. It's like hearing nails on a chalkboard. I quickly retort that music is simply music with no color attached.

People in general need to be more culturally aware but especially our young people. We can't isolate ourselves from the rest of the world because the rest of the world resides everywhere we exist. We can no longer think we are living in an all American society because we don't. Our young people have to know how to interact with people of all races, ethnicities, sexual orientations, ages etcetera. As a society, we set them up for failure if we don't. If you can only function in a world with people who look like you and sound like you then just around the corner a rude awakening is coming.

IF IT'S GOOD UP THERE THEN

IT'S GOOD EVERYWHERE

Having a peaceful state of mind is essential even when faced with life's greatest challenges. Panicking and being on the edge isn't going to help the situation or make it go away. I told a friend, "If it's good up there then its good everywhere" when she was feeling out of sorts. My philosophy is if I can remain calm and keep a level head I can move through any situation. When I'm feeling a bit of stress or pressure about something, I take a mental vacation to some tropical beach location. I'm usually wearing a t-shirt, cut off shorts, and flip flops. It's actually a picture I hold in my head as I become an entrepreneur. I'm looking forward to that beach life. Good mental health is so important but most people take for granted that it will take care of itself. Your brain it just like any other muscle in your body, you have to exercise it, feed it with good nutrition if you want to maximize its potential. I was teaching a group of detained young men about self-sufficiency when out of the blue one of them said, "How do you increase your mind power?" I thought about it for a minute and said, "Through meditation." Take some time to increase your mind power by practicing good mental health exercises like meditation.

#360

YOU DON'T KNOW WHAT YOU'RE

CAPABLE OF UNTIL YOU DO IT

If you're afraid to try something that will get you closer to your dreams then you will never know what you're capable of doing. Don't continue to sit around wondering what it would be like to pursue your dreams. Don't waste energy visualizing the better life if you're too afraid to do something to move closer to it. Think about it for a moment, what is the worst case scenario if you try it and it doesn't work. There are plenty of successful people in this world who tried something and it didn't work the first time. Keep trying until something happens because giving up just isn't an option.

#361

ANYTHING IS POSSIBLE

IF YOU BELIEVE IT

If you believe you can accomplish
something then you can do it. All too often we
don't receive messages in our society that anything
is possible. We are so bogged down with negative
messaging and images that we start to believe it.
We have to be strong and fight against those things
that don't uplift and inspire us to be great. Growing
up, in my head I knew anything was possible but I
didn't believe it in my heart. It wasn't until I started
to experience and overcome life's hardships that I
knew anything was possible. It takes a strong
person to weather life's challenges to come out
victorious on the other side. Sometimes I don't
think we give ourselves enough credit in knowing
that we can persevere through the challenges. We
have to learn to stack up those challenges we moved
through because that is an achievement. Getting
through tough times counts for something so don't
dismiss what you've been through, use it as a
catalyst to push you forward and upward.

SELF-EVALUATION IS NECESSARY

This book as well as the next book is a perspective of my own self-evaluation. Through writing I was able to look inside myself to understand more about the woman who stood before me in the mirror. Both of my books are about awareness, healing, and transformation. I was able to accomplish all three by using my words and examining my thoughts. It was a very therapeutic process and it saved me a lot of money from having to see a therapist. However, I did spend a pretty penny at the university getting a psychology degree so I should have gleaned some insight of self. I am a huge advocate of therapy but I simply chose a route that worked best for me. I didn't realize how therapeutic writing was until now as I type these words. I use to journal when I was a pre-teen and my mother found and read my journal so that ended my days of writing anything down. It wasn't until 2002 I began to write down some thoughts, and ultimately it became the first book I started to write. Some may ask why has it taken so long to write the book. Well the short answer is I was still living the art of what I wanted to say. My young mentee told me I was living the art of my work so be patient and don't have any expectations of finishing any sooner than necessary. Young people are so wise, that's why I love being around them. I'm putting some

final touches on the book and it will be released in
the fall of 2017.

#363

THERE ARE TIMES IN YOUR LIFE WHEN PEOPLE ARE AROUND AND TIMES IN YOUR LIFE WHEN IT'S JUST YOU

What do you do in those times when it's just you? Life seems more vibrant and juicy when people are around. A friend and I would reminiscence about how much fun we had in our thirties and how quiet things became in our forties. We both experienced personal set-backs and challenges that made us stronger and lean a little harder on God. We came into a higher understanding of life and self. We are going into our fifties co-creating our lives with God and living our purpose as He intended.

Teens...people around

Twenties...people around

Thirties...people around

Forties...just me

Fifties…people around and just me

#364

ASCENSION

A special message for my readers...

Before you can ascend to higher heights you must first **crawl** around in the awareness of you. When a baby is trying to take its first steps it wobbles, stumbles, and falls. Like many adults do when trying to pursue their dreams. At some point you will find a solid foundation to **stand** on, and then you begin to **walk** in search of your truth. Don't **run** through the process because the life lessons will unfold. Allow the wind to catch your wings so you can **fly** and **soar** beyond anything you can imagine.

#365

IN MY MOTHER'S WOMB

God had a conversation with me as I lay snuggled in my mother's womb.

Me: "God, who am I?"

God: "You are a child of the Most High which whom much is given, much is required."

Me: "God, what am I supposed to do with my life?"

God: "Your purpose is to elevate the consciousness of humanity using your words. You are a teacher, you are a healer, and you are a life changer."

ABOUT THE AUTHOR

Loronda C. Giddens is an Army veteran who worked as a corporate professional for 13 years before transitioning to state government. She is an experienced human services professional with a strong background in mental health counseling, case management, and substance abuse prevention. Loronda has an extensive history of working with at-risk youth in group homes and the juvenile justice system. Giddens worked as a Juvenile Probation Specialist for 7 years, and currently works as a Victim Advocate with the Georgia Department of Juvenile Justice.

Loronda went from training large corporations on financial services to becoming a P.O.S.T. Certified Instructor. She is a national conference speaker who educates on domestic minor sex trafficking, gender violence, child sexual abuse prevention, bullying, teen dating violence, and LGBTQ awareness. Loronda is Chairperson of Work Group 4: Keeping At-Risk Youth Safe on the Georgia Statewide Human Trafficking Task Force.

Giddens earned a Bachelor's degree in Social Science from the University of Alabama and a Master's degree in Forensic Psychology from Argosy University. She is a self-published author of "Peeling Back the Layers of Your Life: A Pathway Revealing 365 Hidden Treasures" and "Peeling Back the Layers of Your Life: Inspiring Quotes to Live By." Loronda is also Founder of EnerPeace Creations, a business that provides training and speaking services to an array of organizations.

Contact Information

Twitter: @inspired2peel

Instagram: @inspired2peel

Website: www.lorondacgiddens.com

Email: inspired2peel@gmail.com

Made in the USA
Middletown, DE
09 April 2017